THE GOOD LIVING GUIDE TO

HEALING DRINKS

THE GOOD LIVING GUIDE TO

HEALING DRINKS

JUICES, SMOOTHIES, BROTHS & HERBAL TEAS

JENNIFER BROWNE

Photographs by Chrissy Courtney

Good Books

New York, New York

Good Books books may be purchased in bulk at special discounts for sales
promotion, corporate gifts, fund-raising, or educational purposes. Special editions
can also be created to specifications. For details, contact the Special Sales
Department, Good Books, 307 West 36th Street, 11th Floor, New York, NY 10018
or info@skyhorsepublishing.com.

Good Books is an imprint of Skyhorse Publishing, Inc®, a Delaware corporation.

Visit our website at www.goodbooks.com

10 9 8 7 6 5 4 3 2 1

Library of Congress Cataloging-in-Publication Data is available on file.

Cover design by Kai
Cover photo by Chrissy Courtney

Print ISBN: 978-1-68099-926-6
eBook ISBN: 978-1-68099-941-9

Printed in China

Dedication

For those yearning for simpler, more honest, and effective ways
to soothe, strengthen, and restore our bodies.
Food is always the answer, isn't it?

For my wildly entertaining husband who will drink anything
I put before him.
I will always adore you.

Contents

INTRODUCTION

It's the Simple Things

It's amazing how the things that truly heal us are typically cheap and easy to obtain. They come naturally, and there are zero side effects. They're inexpensive, and they're familiar. Whole food, movement, hugs. Walking barefoot outdoors. Cuddling a pet, stretching, humming, smiling. Making eye contact with someone. Sunshine. All these things are healing, promote restoration, and exemplify true intention.

They just feel good.

How we choose to view and utilize medicine is no different. We are often told that medicine is what we find in pharmacies or drug stores, but what we discover there can often be the exact opposite of cheap, easily obtainable, and natural—and there are often side effects. What did we do before retail stores sold us cures that sometimes don't really seem to cure at all? What did we do to soothe, strengthen, and restore our bodies from the often normal and natural ailments that afflict us periodically in life?

We turned to food.

Once upon a time, pharmacies as we know them today did not exist. Human beings had a more intimate relationship with the land and earth where they lived and foraged and there was deep knowledge and respect for the natural resources the earth provided. I'm not talking about fossil fuels or other forms of energy. I'm referring to indigenous plants that grew in harmony with the nature surrounding them. These plants were studied by our ancestors and used wisely for anything from curing sickness and attending to injury, to energy restoration and pain reduction in childbirth. Unfortunately, we now mostly use pharmaceuticals for these ailments and afflictions—and the results are often not the same. Yes, iron supplements can assist with anemia, but so can consuming beetroot.[1] Dimenhydrinate (the medically active ingredient in Gravol) is excellent at reducing fever, but so is ginger.[2] And the thing is this: pharmaceuticals cost more and often have unwanted side effects. Iron supplements can be lethal in large doses and are known to cause constipation, while beet consumption results in neither of these things. Dimenhydrinate is known to make you sleepy, but ginger doesn't do that.

My intention is not to throw shade at medicine that is proven to help heal and work a lot of magic. (I mean, thank goodness for antibiotics and most vaccinations, am I right?) But natural, good, easily accessible, healthy, and nourishing food is the absolute foundation of good health and your biggest ally in the fight against chronic disease. We know this, and we can do better. Choose better. Because we *deserve* better. Make more informed and educational decisions regarding our health and that of our families.

We're only here for a finite amount of time, so why not live our best lives in bodies that function optimally?

Why Drinks?

Food is medicine that our bodies recognize and respond easily and quickly to. It nourishes us from the inside out, and drinks are easy to digest and simple to travel or move around with. They're also easier to ingest when we're suffering from ailments such as nausea, or when we're not hungry because we have a cold. Think of teas brewed with herbs from your very own garden, fresh-pressed juices designed to flood our bodies with nature's goodness, thick blended smoothies full of medicinal plants, hearty life-affirming broths, nutritive plant-based mylks, and herbal tonics and coolers that help to restore our bodies to homeostasis. The healing drinks in this book are easily and intentionally concocted with information that your body recognizes and can naturally respond to. We've all heard the term "food is medicine," but what if we thought of food as information? And what if we took the time to regularly audit this information for accuracy and effectiveness? Drinks are often the afterthought when it comes to meal planning and preparation, but *healing* drinks are a great supplement to one's weekly menu and can often be the meal itself depending on your current circumstances.

Why this Book?

In *The Good Living Guide to Medicinal Tea*, I wrote about how to make simple teas that can cure what ails you—but tea should not have the entire spotlight. There are many drinks we can concoct with the same intention as the teas in that book, including recipes such as Fresh-Pressed Beet Juice for iron deficiency, Citrus Ginger Smoothie for immune health, and Floral Cooler for skin clarity. In *The Good Living Guide to Healing Drinks*, you will learn about fifty whole foods that can solve fifty of our most common complaints, complete with usage, recipes, and preservation tips. These foods make delicious and effective drinks that contain all the necessary components to heal and promote healthy growth—but let's get specific.

Part One is divided into six sections. It includes helpful information on plant-based mylks (accompanied by three of my favorite recipes), bone broth, kefir and kombucha (the misfits), and adaptogenic mushrooms. It also covers the topics of preservation and storage of herbs, how and when to use sweeteners, and includes a list of kitchen equipment I find personally useful when making the healing recipes found in this book.

Part Two includes a glossary of medicinal terms associated with healing foods that one may find helpful, a section about whole foods and their general benefits in contrast to foods that are heavily processed, and it lists the fifty foods that I find so personally valuable when it comes to making our healing drinks. These foods are the core ingredients for all fifty recipes associated with the fifty common ailments that we cover in depth in Part Three.

Part Three presents these fifty common afflictions in detail, gives a brief description of the different types of elixirs featured in this book, and of course, includes the fifty recipes that are so valuable when added to our wellness regimens. Each recipe indicates whether its main purpose is to soothe, strengthen, or restore, but keep in mind that all these recipes provide a combination of these three things in some form.

I encourage you to experiment with these recipes and make them your own. Add, dilute, and enhance these offerings and find out what works best for you. Come home to your body by way of informative food in the form of healing drinks that will serve you in so many therapeutic ways.

Cheers to drinking yourself healthy, my friends.

Part One: Big Picture Basics

Plant-Based Mylks

Plant-based mylks can easily be purchased at almost any grocery store these days. They've gained major traction in the last decade or so and have come a long way in terms of taste and overall quality. These mylks usually contain preservatives that increase shelf life, which can be a pro or con depending on your priorities and your family's weekly mylk consumption.

Personally, I'm an advocate for making your own mylks when you can—which is a big deal, because it does take some time and planning. Nevertheless, learning the process, making a recipe your own, and perfecting the skill of making homemade mylk is an art. It's wildly satisfying, and it gives you control over the quality of ingredients. It's also typically more cost effective (especially if you and your family are consuming a lot), and it strengthens the connection between you and your food.

The following plant-based mylks are the ones used in this book. Some of the recipes in this book call for ready-made mylks, and some have the mylk making incorporated into the recipes themselves. If you decide to make the mylks in these recipes yourself, here are the recipes I love to use. Feel free to play around, mix up spices, and add whatever you feel your body needs in the moment. Maybe you add some turmeric or cloves—it's one hundred percent your call.

ALMOND MYLK

Almond mylk is probably one of the more popular plant-based mylks out there. It's highly diverse, it has a mild and pleasant flavor, and it's widely available. Here is my own recipe for slightly sweetened almond mylk:

Ingredients:
1 cup raw, unsalted almonds
5 cups filtered water
2 whole pitted dates
1 teaspoon vanilla extract
1 pinch sea salt

Method:
Soak almonds overnight in cool water, or for 2–3 hours in hot water. Add your soaked almonds, water, dates (make sure they're pitted!), vanilla, and salt to a high-speed blender and blend for about 1–2 minutes until creamy and smooth. Strain mixture into a bowl using a nut mylk bag, cheesecloth, or thin dish towel. Transfer milk to a jar or covered bottle and refrigerate for up to 4–5 days. Shake before using, as plant-based mylks tend to separate.

Tip: Use leftover almond pulp to throw into baking or overnight oats.

Cashew Mylk

Cashew mylk tends to be a little thicker than almond mylk. I prefer this mylk when I want something creamy, and it also produces no leftover pulp because it doesn't need to be strained—it blends beautifully.

Ingredients:
1 cup raw, unsalted cashews
4 cups filtered water
1 tablespoon pure maple syrup
1 teaspoon vanilla extract
1 pinch sea salt

Method:
Soak cashews overnight in cool water, or for 2 hours in hot water. Add your soaked cashews, water, maple syrup, vanilla, and salt to a high-speed blender and blend for about 1–2 minutes until creamy and smooth. Transfer mylk directly into jar or covered bottle (no need to strain) and refrigerate for up to 4–5 days. Shake before using.

Tip: If you choose to use salted cashews, omit the sea salt.

OAT MYLK

Oat mylk is so easy to make and is the foundation for all my super yummy lattes. It's also comforting in a weird kind of nostalgic way. I didn't drink oat mylk growing up, but for some reason I find it very sentimental. (I mean, I ate a lot of oatmeal . . .)

Ingredients:
½ cup whole (preferably sprouted) rolled oats
3 cups filtered water
½ tablespoon raw, unpasteurized honey (optional)
1 teaspoon cinnamon
1 pinch sea salt

Method:
Combine all ingredients in a high-speed blender and blend for about 1 minute. Place a fine mesh strainer over a bowl and strain the milk without pushing any excess oat pulp through the strainer. Transfer mylk directly into jar or covered bottle and chill before drinking. This will keep in the refrigerator for up to 2–3 days. Shake before using, as oat mylk separates.

Bone Broth, Kefir, and Kombucha

There are three very healing drinks that I haven't provided recipes for in this book, but nevertheless, I feel they deserve their very own shoutout. Bone broth, kefir, and kombucha are all highly nutritious in their own ways for their own reasons, but their main ingredients are not foods that I've chosen to list in this book—this does not mean you should avoid them. There are specific ingredients in each that may irritate someone who is sensitive to what makes them nutritionally invaluable to others, so you'll need to figure out where you fall on that spectrum. Bone broth is obviously made from animal protein, so if you're vegan or eat primarily plant-based, you'll want to avoid it. Kefir is dairy based, so if you're sensitive to dairy or your body has a lot of inflammation, skip it. Lastly, kombucha is full of amazing digestive enzymes that help the gut build good bacteria and create better homeostasis. However, if you experience a lot of digestive issues or are sensitive to carbonation, then this may not be the healing drink for you.

Let's just take a deeper dive into what bone broth, kefir, and kombucha are exactly, and why you should consider incorporating them into your healing plan.

BONE BROTH

While I think bone broth can be a beneficial drink, I mostly stick to a plant-based diet and so don't often have bones on hand to make my own. Even if I did, I've never made it myself and wouldn't be the best resource for ideas on this task. Local butchers would be great places to source quality bones, and in the spirit of using and consuming all parts of an animal if one chooses to use any, I would start here, first.

So, what is bone broth exactly? At its essence, it's a light soup or broth made from the bones and connective tissue of any animal. Humans have been making bone broth since the days of cavepeople, and the drink has a multitude of nutritional benefits including the following:

- Very high in collagen (supports joint and bone health)
- Protein rich (typically over 9 grams per serving)
- Easy on the digestive system and aids in leaky gut syndrome
- Supports wound healing and improves skin elasticity
- Teeming with electrolytes, vitamins, and minerals

This nourishing elixir is a great example of the kinds of foods that should be offered in a hospital or wellness environment, post-surgery. When your body must heal and your energy is depleted and you need to be warmed from the inside out with nutrients that are clearly comprehensible and instructive to your body, this is the time for a healing drink like bone broth. Again, it's not included in this book, but I felt it important enough to discuss at length.

KEFIR

Kefir is a fermented dairy product known for its generous prebiotic and probiotic properties. Think of it as a thin yogurt made from kefir grains. Touted as highly nutritious, it's best known for its ability to improve digestion, lower cholesterol, and manage blood sugar. In this way, it can be viewed as a healing drink for metabolic disease. It's also proven to be antimicrobial, anticancer, and antidiabetic.[1]

I didn't include kefir in the main list of healing drinks in this book because it's usually dairy based, which so many people find inflammatory. Although recognized by the general health community as beneficial, it's not for everyone.

KOMBUCHA

Kombucha is a fermented healing drink that wasn't included in the bulk of this book, because it's a combination of several ingredients that make it beneficial to one's health: it's made with tea, sugar, bacteria, and yeast. The resulting product contains vinegar, B vitamins, and several other chemical compounds and produces a fizzy, mildly vinegar-flavored drink that's an oddly appealing symbiotic culture of bacteria and yeast. Like kefir, this carbonated drink offers a whole host of gastrointestinal benefits and is known to be antioxidant, antimicrobial, antidiabetic, and anticancer.[2]

Kombucha comes in a whole range and variety of flavors and is typically sold in the refrigerated section of grocery or health food stores. Some people experience mild digestive distress when consuming kombucha, as it can initially lead to increased gas and bloating. If you've never tried kombucha before, I recommend starting off with small amounts that your body can process well before increasing the volume you consume.

ADAPTOGENIC MUSHROOMS

Mushrooms are one of the foods featured in this book, but there is a distinct difference between the common mushroom and the adaptogenic ones we use in healing recipes. Although regular cooking mushrooms (such as white button, cremini, portobello, oyster, morel, and porcini) are very healthful and contain good quantities of protein, selenium, and a plethora of vitamins, the adaptogenic varieties are generally superior and are the ones that have been used in functional medicine for thousands of years. Hippocrates, universally recognized as the father of modern medicine, used adaptogenic mushrooms for wound healing and anti-inflammatory purposes.[1]

In recent years, adaptogenic mushrooms have become quite popular and mainstream again within the health food industry. Although they have been used widely in homeopathic remedies for ages and are easy to spot in functional pharmacies and naturopathic centers, these mushrooms can now be commonly found as ingredients in tinctures, teas, tonics, and supplements almost everywhere. Why are adaptogenic mushrooms so popular now? Probably because we're paying more attention and rediscovering what our ancestors knew a very long time ago: mushrooms can contain deep reservoirs of powerful medicines. We're also learning more about them as a species, which is probably making us more comfortable. Humans have traditionally been wary of mushrooms for good reason: they have the ability to heal us, feed us, kill us, and propel us into short-term spiritual journeys.

What other species of plant have such diverse abilities?

In this book, we refer to adaptogenic mushrooms that are proven to be the healing kind. These include lion's mane, reishi, chaga, turkey tail, shitake, maitake, and cordyceps mushrooms. Wild turkey tail is by far the most attractive and fascinating to study, and the gorgeous and distinct mushrooms pictured here were actually foraged by this book's photographer from her very own backyard.

You will read and learn more about the specific healing properties of adaptogenic mushrooms in Part Two.

Preservation and Storage of Herbs

Herb: /(h)ərb/ (*noun*)
Any plant with leaves, seeds, or flowers used for flavoring, food, medicine, or perfume.

There are several medicinal herbs mentioned in this book that play a central role in some of the recipes listed. These herbs can all be easily grown at home, purchased through an herb supplier, or even found at your local health food store. If you're using fresh herbs for the cooler and tonic recipes and have leftovers, I suggest preserving them so you can use them later for teas.

Drying is the simplest method of preserving herbs, and the only one I really use. Simply expose the herbs to warm, dry air. Leave them in a well-ventilated area until all moisture in them completely evaporates. Note that sun drying is not recommended because the herbs can lose flavor and color, and depending on where you live, it's often too humid. Too much humidity can make the herbs rot or mold, so dry air is best.

The best time to harvest most herbs for drying is just before the flowers first open when they are in the bursting bud stage. Gather the herbs in the early morning after the dew has evaporated to minimize wilting. Rinse the herbs in cool water and gently shake to remove excess moisture. Discard all bruised, rotten, or imperfect leaves and stems.

Hearty herbs such as rosemary, sage, thyme, and parsley are the easiest to dry, in my opinion. Tie them into small bundles and hang them to air dry in your kitchen to make the space smell incredible. Basil, oregano, tarragon, lemon balm, and peppermint have a high moisture content and will mold if not dried quickly. You can try using a dehydrator for these herbs, since the temperature will be controlled, and you are guaranteed no moisture. Dried leaves may be left whole and crumpled as used, or coarsely crumpled before storage. Husks can be removed from seeds by rubbing the seeds between the hands and blowing away the chaff. Place herbs in airtight containers and store in a cool, dry, dark area to protect color and fragrance (I typically use glass jars with tight fitting lids). Keep in mind that dried herbs are usually about three to four times stronger than fresh herbs, which is important when making healing drinks.

Here are the herbs used in healing drink recipes in this book, along with the parts of the plant that are commonly consumed. I've included a few foods, such as rose and vanilla, that are not herbs but do provide healing benefits as well as flavor:

Basil (leaf)

Cayenne (fruit)

Chamomile (flower, bud, leaf)

Cinnamon (bark)

Dandelion (flower, root, stem, leaf)

Echinacea (flower, root, leaf)

Ginkgo (nut)

Ginseng (root)

Green tea (leaf)

Hibiscus (flower)

Hops (flower, shoot)

Lavender (flower)

Lemongrass (stalk)

Parsley (stem, leaf)

Peppermint (leaf)

Rose (flower)

Rosemary (leaf, twig)

Thyme (flower, leaf)

Turmeric (root)

Vanilla (pod, seed)

SWEETENERS

Lastly, let's take a good hard look at sugar. You'll notice that in some of the healing drink recipes, there is a sweetener included. Sometimes it's marked optional (if you like your drinks sweet, add it) and sometimes it's not (because without it, the drink might be unpalatable). Either way, note that the sweeteners listed are either stevia, raw and unpasteurized honey, or pure maple syrup. Honey is also one of the fifty healing foods listed in this book, so it gets a lot of acknowledgments.

Regular table sugar (white sugar) has no health benefits at all. It contributes to glucose spikes, irregular insulin dumps, and your body will ultimately store it as fat when you eat too much (which is easier than you think). Overconsumption of refined and heavily processed sugar is known to cause a whole host of problems, including increasing risk for insulin resistance and type 2 diabetes, cardiovascular disease, cancer, undesired weight gain, metabolic disorders, chronic fatigue, and more.[1] Adding refined sugar to the recipes would basically undermine all the wellness benefits we're trying to reap by consuming healing drinks. Please don't do this!

On the next pages you'll see why stevia, raw and unpasteurized honey, and pure maple syrup are the better sweetener alternatives that I've chosen to include in this book.

STEVIA

Stevia is an herb native to South America. It's become quite popular due to the fact that its leaves are a stronger sweetener than sucralose (refined table sugar) but contain no calories. It's also low on the glycemic index, making it suitable for diabetics to use. In addition to its hypoglycemic property, the plant also exhibits antibacterial, anti-inflammatory, hypotensive, antiseptic, diuretic, anti-fertility, and cardiotonic properties.[2] It has also been documented to display positive effects on treating skin diseases such as dermatitis, acne, and eczema.[3] Stevia is incredibly sweet, so it's best to use sparingly.

Although I tend to gravitate towards stevia when in need of a little sweetness, it's worth noting that it has been found to be an endocrine disruptor and so may not be suitable for all. For example, if you know you suffer from adrenal issues, perhaps swap it for raw honey or pure maple syrup.

Raw and Unpasteurized Honey

In ancient civilizations, honey was used for both nutritional and medical purposes, and has been viewed as a nutrient, a medicine, and an ointment. To reap as many benefits as possible, honey in its purest, unrefined, and unprocessed form should be used. Raw and unpasteurized honey is known to be incredibly antibacterial, antimicrobial, antibiotic, and anti-inflammatory.[4] It's traditionally been used for wound-healing, gut health improvement, skin care, infection, and allergy treatment and prevention. Manuka honey has even been reported to exhibit antimicrobial activity against aggressive pathogenic bacteria such as *Staphylococcus aureus* (*S. aureus*) and *Helicobacter pylori* (*H. pylori*), making this honey a promising functional food for the treatment of serious wounds and stomach ulcers.[5] Honey provides a smooth ride in recipes, so it's one of my favorites to use as a complement to some of the healing drinks.

PURE MAPLE SYRUP

Pure maple syrup is not only high in antioxidants, but also offers nutrients like riboflavin, magnesium, calcium, zinc, and potassium. When compared to other natural sweeteners, maple syrup is believed to be preferable because of its high concentration of phenolic compounds and mineral content.[6] It's been found to be anti-mutagenic, anti-radical, antioxidant, and anti-cancer, and brings about lower glucose and insulin responses.[7] Because of its unique and warming fragrance and taste, pure maple syrup is a delicious sugar alternative and perfect for adding to plant-based mylks.

Kitchen Equipment for Making Healing Drinks

Not everyone will have everything on this list of equipment that I use to make the drinks in this book—and that's okay. There are always workarounds, and I will mention them when I can. I don't personally own everything I used, either. The book's photographer supplied the juicer, the espresso maker is my husband's pride and joy (I don't know how to use it aside from steaming milk, so I can't claim to own it), and other bits and pieces were lent to me so I could make everything properly.

The following is a short list of favorite equipment that I used to make the drinks in this book. Don't fret if you don't have it all; none of us do.

- **Canning jars and lids:** For storage of dried herbs, as well as fresh juices, broths, tonics, mylks, and coolers. The lids are an important part, because then you can shake a fresh juice or mylk that has separated a bit after a couple of days in the fridge. You can usually find a flat of inexpensive jars with lids at your local dollar or thrift store.
- **Cheesecloth or nut mylk bag:** Cheesecloth is great for straining nut and oat mylks, but also helpful for straining herbs from tea. Nut mylk bags are specifically for making your own plant-based mylks and I would highly recommend investing in one if you make a lot. But honestly? I mostly use worn dishtowels.
- **Espresso machine:** This gem is totally optional and by far the most expensive and privileged piece of kitchen equipment on this list. But, if you do own one, they're great for making incredible coffee and usually come with a steamer for steaming mylks.

- **High-powered blender**: I use a Vitamix, but any high-powered blender will do. I emphasize "high-powered" simply because they do a much better job of blending nuts and oats into a smooth and creamy liquid. Sometimes the more inexpensive blenders don't do as well with this but will still do an excellent job with the average smoothie. Use what you have.
- **Infusing tea pot**: You'll see mine in a few of this book's photos. These are great when you're making tea with dried herb blends because you can add the herbs directly into a little cup that sits within the pot while steeping. Once done, you simply remove the little cup—no mess and no fuss.
- **Juicer**: Necessary for making fresh-pressed juices. No other piece of equipment works well for this. If you think you'll be juicing a lot, these are a solid investment for your health.
- **Kettle**: Again, necessary for heating water. Unless you have access to instant hot water, and then I'm just plain jealous . . .
- **Knives**: I recommend one or two great paring knives, as well as a variety of others. Anything sharp (and not serrated) will do.

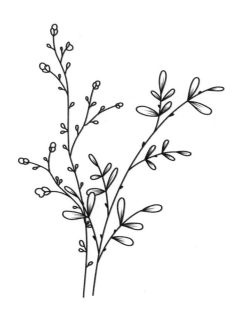

Part Two: 50 Foods that Soothe, Strengthen, and Restore

When we think of food as information, we can quickly start to categorize it. Pretend you have buckets in front of you, and you're grouping foods that you think are similar in each of the buckets. You may have a bucket for grains, a bucket for meat, one for dairy, and one for fruit. You probably have a vegetable bucket, and perhaps a bucket of confections. Then within those buckets, you can further divide the foods. From the grains bucket, you can separate processed grains from whole grains. In the fruit bucket, you could separate locally grown fruit from fruit that must be imported. Maybe the dairy bucket gets separated into low-fat and full fat. What we have here is a lot of choice, and we can choose to consume food in certain buckets and leave the other buckets alone. Further, we can choose to only consume certain *segments* of each bucket.

Each food that is discussed in this book would come from a portion of a bucket that is highly nutritious, and full of information your body can process and understand. They're part of a highly narrowed down group of foods that are worthy of being consumed by your body—and in this section of the book, we're going to learn why.

Glossary of Medicinal Terms

This second section of this book focuses on foods that heal. Whether they're used preventatively or acutely, these foods contain important components that lead to optimal health and wellness. Many of the terms used to describe these foods will be familiar, but some may not. Here is the collection of medicinal terms that we use in this book, along with corresponding descriptions to familiarize yourself with and refer to:

Adaptogen: a natural substance used in herbal medicine to normalize and regulate the systems of the body.

Analgesic: pain-relieving.

Anti-aging: effective in slowing or stopping the effects of aging.

Antiallergenic: non-aggravating to an allergy, and unlikely to cause an allergic reaction.

Anti-apoptotic: a function that suppresses apoptosis and autophagy, which is used widely in therapy resistance against multiple types of cancer.

Anti-asthmatic: something that relieves or reduces the symptoms of asthma.

Antibacterial: destructive to or inhibiting the growth of bacteria.

Antibiotic: chemical substances (such as penicillin) produced by various microorganisms and fungi, which have the capacity to inhibit the growth of or to destroy bacteria and other microorganisms. Used primarily in the treatment of infectious diseases.

Anticancer: anything that is proven effective in the treatment of cancer.

Anticonvulsant: an agent used to treat epileptic seizures.

Antidepressant: a substance used to relieve depression (and usually anxiety).

Antidiabetic: herbs or medicines used to stabilize and manage diabetes.

Antiemetic: a substance or agent that suppresses nausea and/or vomiting.

Antifungal: inhibiting the growth of fungi.

Antihypertensive: commonly used in the treatment of high blood pressure.

Anti-infective: substances used to help fight infection.

Anti-inflammatory: acting to reduce certain signs of inflammation, as swelling, tenderness, fever, and pain.

Antilipemic: limits number of lipids in the blood.

Antimicrobial: destructive to or inhibiting the growth of microorganisms.

Antimutative: a substance that supports healthy cells and inhibits or prevents atypical mutation.

Antioxidant: substances that protect your cells against free radical (cancer-causing) agents.

Antiparasitic: killing or inhibiting growth of parasites.

Antiplatelet: substances that prevent blood clots from forming.

Antirheumatic: helps to relieve occurrences and symptoms of rheumatism.

Antispasmodic: helps to prevent and relieve muscle spasms and cramping.

Antithrombotic: a drug or herbal medicine that reduces the formation of blood clots.

Aperient: possessing a purgative or laxative affect.

Aromatic: fragrant; smells good.

Cleanser: a substance or agent that cleans and purifies the body.

Cytoprotective: a substance that protects against gastric mucosal injury.

Depressant: possessing the sedative quality of depressing or lowering vital activities.

Detoxifier: a substance or agent that rids one of poisons and/or toxins, or the effects of such.

Diaphoretic: produces perspiration.

Diuretic: increasing urine excretion.

Estrogenic: promoting or producing estrogen.

Expectorant: promoting the discharge of phlegm or other fluid from the respiratory tract.

Galactagogue: an herb that promotes, stimulates, and/or increases lactation.

Hepatoprotective: the ability of a substance to prevent damage or injury to the liver.

Hypolipidemic: a substance that lowers the concentrations of agents that transport cholesterol in the bloodstream.

Hypoglycemic: refers to a state of low blood sugar, or when the levels of glucose in your bloodstream drop significantly.

Hypotensive: blood pressure reducing.

Immunomodulatory: treats diseases that plague the immune system.

Immunostimulant: anything that enhances the non-specific immune response by interacting directly with cells of the system activating them.

Laxative: a substance that relieves constipation.

Neuroprotective: mechanisms and strategies employed to defend the central nervous system.

Purgative: a cathartic medicine or agent; stimulating waste evacuation from the bowels.

Sedative: a substance that calms and/or soothes.

Stimulant: something that quickens the functional activity of some organ or part.

Tonic: a healthy substance that strengthens or invigorates.

The Whole (Food) Story

Whole foods have a purpose. They contain valuable information that, when consumed, supports our bodies in functioning the way they're supposed to. Our bodies identify the information, read it, and use it—or not. Sometimes the information it receives is confusing and unidentifiable and instead of using it for a specific purpose that leads to better health, it deploys an army of defenders that ultimately results in inflammation, which then leads to chronic disease.

What we choose to eat is literally life or death: it can help us soothe, strengthen, and restore, or it can contribute to confusion, breakdown, and disease. When deciding what to put in your mouth, ask yourself these five questions:

- Will my body know what this is?
- Will I feel good after eating this?
- Will this give me energy?
- Would I feed this to a small child?
- Would this be beneficial for someone who is sick?

If you find yourself answering negatively to many of these questions, consider making a different choice. The key is to consistently consume foods that have you answering yes.

The following list of fifty foods is one of beauty. These foods are so full of beneficial components that they are all used for both preventative and acute purposes. They have all been studied and peer reviewed by doctors and scientists. You're probably familiar with most of them and already know some of the information I'm going to share with you. But I bet the health benefits of these foods blow your mind when you find out just how amazing they really are.

Many of the foods listed in this book are either sitting in your fridge, freezer, or pantry—I'm sure of it. Some of them may be more obscure, such as coconut and chlorophyl. But many of them you probably buy on a regular basis, such as cucumber, carrot, and coffee. If you don't have everything on this list of fifty, don't fret. Perhaps making healing drinks can be your excuse to procure something new and exciting.

Are you ready?

Healing Foods

Almond
Aloe
Avocado
Basil
Beetroot
Blueberry
Cacao
Carrot
Cashew
Cayenne
Celery
Chamomile
Chlorophyll
Cinnamon
Coconut
Coffee
Cranberry
Cucumber
Dandelion
Echinacea
Fennel
Flaxseed
Garlic
Ginger
Ginkgo

Ginseng
Grapefruit
Green tea
Hibiscus
Honey
Hops
Kale
Lavender
Lemon
Lemongrass
Matcha
Miso
Mushroom
Oat
Onion
Orange
Parsley
Peppermint
Pineapple
Rose
Rosemary
Thyme
Turmeric
Vanilla
Watermelon

ALMOND

Almonds are not just incredibly delicious when coated in chocolate! Recent clinical studies have confirmed their regulatory effect on body mass index, protective effects against cardiovascular disease and diabetes, and even their prebiotic potential to improve gut health.[1] Studies also suggest almonds play a role in enhancing cognitive performance.[2] The next time you're looking for a snack, try helping yourself to a handful of almonds.

ALOE

Traditionally used as a topical skin treatment for wound healing and tissue recovery, aloe has an impressive number of medicinal properties associated with its use, including being antibacterial, antiviral, antiseptic, and anti-inflammatory.[3] When ingested orally for medicinal purposes, this interesting plant has been proven to help improve blood glucose levels, assist with constipation, treat mild to moderate ulcerative colitis, and even stabilize metastatic cancers.[4]

You can purchase organic, cold-processed aloe vera juice to add to smoothies, coolers, or just plain water. Be sure to use aloe that is processed for consumption; aloe for dermatological health is processed differently.

AVOCADO

Avocados are typically touted for their high fiber and vitamin A content, but a variety of studies have also shown the fruit to be successful at improving cardiovascular health.[5] Other studies suggest that avocados help to support skin health and weight management, as well as offer a diverse array of anti-inflammatory benefits.[6] They also help to stimulate cognitive function and improve overall gut health[7]—total wonder food.

Don't let the high fat content of avocados scare you. Remember that these lovely fruits (yes—technically fruit) are a source of good fat that help you feel fuller for longer. One half of an avocado equals approximately one serving.

BASIL

When I think of basil, my brain goes straight to caprese salads. I love the herb for its fragrant yet gentle leaves and the ease with which it grows in my garden—but the plant is much more than delicious and easy. Traditionally, basil has been used to treat gastrointestinal issues, but the plant's therapeutic potential extends beyond just assisting with an upset stomach. Basil has been shown to be effective in the treatment of certain cancers, in boosting the immune system, and in the reduction of inflammation.[8]

Basil can be used in almost any meal, as well as for sauces, in smoothies, and as an edible garnish for just about any healing drink imaginable.

BEETROOT

For a long time, beetroot has been used as a natural additive in food substances for its dark pink coloring (naturally colored pink cupcake icing, for example). More recently though, the root has been hypothesized and proven to be highly effective in the prevention and treatment of many common health disorders and afflictions, including inhibiting cancerous cell proliferation, lowering blood pressure and blood sugar, enhancing athletic performance, treating muscle soreness, and elevating energy levels.[9] Beetroot, leaf, and stalk is also an excellent natural remedy and treatment for anemia.[10]

BLUEBERRY

These delicious berries may as well be candy, especially when frozen—but they boast a ton of impressive health benefits. They are very high in certain phytochemicals, which are known to help reduce the risk of cardiovascular disease and type 2 diabetes, and they offer neuroprotection to ward off overall risk of degenerative diseases and rapid cellular aging.[11] In other words, these gems provide important health benefits to a variety of our body's major working systems.

Cacao

Cacao is typically used in a variety of processed foodstuffs, but the plant is much more than a source of chocolate. Clinical studies have proven that cacao has the potential to be used for the prevention and treatment of seasonal allergies, certain cancers, oxidative injuries, inflammatory conditions, anxiety, mood, hyperglycemia, and insulin resistance. It also assists in weight management and weight loss.[12] Because of these health benefits, raw cacao makes an excellent addition to smoothies, avocado pudding, and no-bake goodies.

CARROT

Widely known for their ability to help improve vision, carrots are more than meets the eye. They possess multiple nutritional and health benefits, including potential metabolic and cardiovascular protective effects.[13] They contain lots of fiber and assist in lowering blood pressure.[14] The relative popularity of carrot juice is for good reason: it contains high levels of vitamin E, carotenoids, and a host of other micronutrients that boast an impressive nutritive profile.[15] Carrot allergies and/or sensitivities are extremely rare, so they also make an excellent snack both for school and the workplace.

Cashew

Who doesn't love cashews?! They make an incredible base for plant-based cheese, mylks, and sauces and are delicious to munch on their own—but they also contain some serious goodness in the health and wellness department. Cashews are abundant in monounsaturated and polyunsaturated fatty acids, which are closely associated with reduced cardiovascular disease risk.[16] In addition, these fun halfmoon-shaped nuts are known to reduce cholesterol.[17]

Like avocados, they are the perfect example of a healthy fat not to shy away from. Just remember that all nuts are high in calories, so the more is better rule doesn't necessarily work here. Instead, try to consume one quarter cup of cashews (about six nuts) two to three times per week.

CAYENNE

Cayenne is a commonly dried hot chili pepper extract and used in cooking for its spicy flavor—but it's not all about the heat! Cayenne is analgesic (pain relieving) and can help minimize both acute and chronic inflammation.[18] Studies have also shown that this pungent diaphoretic positively affects circulatory and endocrine systems. It aids digestion and assists with healthy weight maintenance and reduction of overall cholesterol and blood fat levels, making it hypolipidemic.[19]

Make sure you wash your hands well after handing cayenne—you don't want to accidentally rub your eyes after touching it.

CELERY

Celery must be one of the most underrated vegetables when it comes to perceived nutritive health benefits. In fact, studies have shown that both stalk and leaf boast a lot of goodness, including vitamin C, antioxidants, beta carotene, and manganese.[20] Celery helps to suppress cardiovascular inflammation, as well as oxidative damage to the blood stream.[21]

The next time you're looking for a quick, healthy, and light snack, consider turning to celery. I like to load it with nut butter for some added protein.

CHAMOMILE

Chamomile is a widely used herb in traditional medicine, which is why you'll often see it as a main ingredient in medicinal teas—especially teas used as sleep or calming aids. Chamomile contains compounds that possess anticancer, anti-infective, anti-inflammatory, antithrombotic, antioxidant, antihypertensive, antidepressant, and neuroprotective activities.[22] This is quite an impressive list!

CHLOROPHYLL

When we eat green fruits and vegetables, we consume chlorophyll. Chlorophyll plays an important role in photosynthesis and is a naturally occurring pigment and bioactive compound found in green colored plants. Studies have shown that chlorophyll is extremely high in antioxidants, as well as being anti-inflammatory, anticancer, beneficial for wound healing, and antimutagenic.[23] Green, leafy lettuces, root greens (such as carrot and beet greens), chard, kale, and mustard greens are some vegetables that are high in chlorophyll. Fruits include kiwis, green grapes, green apple skins, and honeydew.

You can increase the level of chlorophyll you consume by purchasing chlorophyll liquid extract and adding it to smoothies, juices, teas, and even just plain water.

CINNAMON

Cinnamon is one spice that everyone seems to adore. Widely used in baking, sauces, and an additive to dishes like oatmeal and smoothies, it's also teeming with a variety of health benefits. In a systematic review titled *Cinnamon: Mystic Powers of a Minute Ingredient*, researchers concluded that cinnamon has antioxidant, anti-inflammatory, antilipemic, antidiabetic, antimicrobial, and anticancer effects on the human body.[24] Friends . . . that's a lot of antis!

Cinnamon is also warming, which makes it comforting in cool weather or throughout the winter months. It can easily be added to teas for both a boost in flavor and added nutrients.

Coconut

Tropical coconuts are typically a fan favorite. You can consume both the meat and the water directly from a fresh coconut, and coconut mylk and oils are also wildly popular because of the plant's associated health benefits. Coconuts are both delicious and healing!

Coconut is a medium-chain fatty acid with a ton of known medicinal properties. Clinical studies have proven that they help to improve cognitive function and lower blood pressure.[25] They are also antibacterial, antifungal, antiviral, antiparasitic, antioxidant, hypoglycemic, hepatoprotective, and immunostimulant.[26]

COFFEE

Coffee often gets a bad reputation for a few different reasons. One: It contains caffeine, which is officially classified as a drug for its stimulant properties. Two: It is dehydrating and can stain teeth. However, studies have shown it has a long list of health benefits, so don't ditch it quite yet!

In several clinical studies, coffee has been proven to contribute to the prevention of oxidative stress and inflammatory related diseases, such as type 2 diabetes, obesity, and metabolic syndrome. Its consumption is also associated with a lower risk of several types of cancer and a reduction of general mortality.[27]

CRANBERRY

Cranberries may be tart, but they sure carry a lot of goodness! Heavy in various types of bioactive compounds associated with wellness, cranberries have long been recognized for their positive effects on urinary tract health.[28] They also carry health benefits associated with oral and vascular health, as well as antimicrobial, antibacterial, and antioxidant properties.[29]

Since the fruit is sour, common ways to consume cranberries include the addition of sugar. I would deter you from going that route, however, since sugar is inflammatory and is known to feed cancer cells.[30] Instead, unsweetened cranberry juice or cranberry powder is better. I personally prefer to take cranberry powder in veggie capsule supplement form, or I juice the fresh or previously frozen berries myself. I also love cranberry tea.

CUCUMBER

Not surprisingly, cucumber belongs to the same family as melon, squash, and pumpkins. It is high in water content and low in calories, which is why it makes a great snack for both kids and adults alike. It produces a cleansing action within the body by removing accumulated pockets of old waste materials and chemical toxins. Cucumber also contains antidiabetic, lipid lowering, and antioxidant activity.[31]

Fresh cucumber juice is often used for nourishing the skin, whether it be via oral consumption or topical treatment. When consumed for medicinal purposes, cucumber is often juiced. When used topically, it gives a soothing effect against skin irritations and reduces swelling, which is why you're probably familiar with it being used to reduce bags under the eyes. Cucumber also can relax and alleviate painful sunburns—not unlike its good friend, aloe.

DANDELION

More than just an attractive yellow weed, dandelion is brimming with functional health benefits that have been proven by clinical studies for decades. The plant can be consumed in salads, roasted with vegetables, and are a common ingredient in medicinal teas. The root can be used as a for a caffeine-free alternative to coffee, the leaves are often eaten raw in salads (lending a slightly pleasant bitterness), and simple syrups are commonly made from the flowers. It is an herb that is just as much a medicinal agent as it is a food!

Dandelion possesses antioxidant and anti-inflammatory activities that result in positive and diverse biological effects on the human body. Its leaves are known to be a rich source of potassium, and the whole plant is used for the treatment of type 2 diabetes, atherosclerosis, and metabolic syndrome. Dandelion also helps to regulate lipid and carbohydrate metabolism.[32] It is nature's gift, and it grows easily and quickly across a very large portion of the world.

ECHINACEA

Echinacea (you'd probably recognize the purple coneflower) is widely used as an herbal medicine for those who are sick with a cold or experiencing chest congestion and inflammation. Typically consumed in tea and tincture forms, this herb is proven to assist with the treatment of respiratory tract infections, coughs, colds, and various inflammatory conditions.[33] The plant consists of antibacterial, antimicrobial, anti-inflammatory, and antioxidant properties that do an excellent job of nursing one back to good health.[34] Echinacea tea is one of my favorite teas to drink during the fall and winter to both prevent and treat the common cold.

FENNEL

Fresh fennel is one of my absolute favorite things to add to salad, fish, and chicken dishes. Its anise flavor is distinct and delicious, and I secretly love how the cashier at my local grocery store always has no idea what it is.

Fennel extract is known to possess anti-inflammatory, antibacterial, antifungal, antioxidant, antiviral, and immunomodulatory effects.[35] Studies have also confirmed its anti-apoptotic and cytoprotective features.[36] You can also use fennel seed or dried fennel in teas, broths, and other types of warming elixirs.

FLAXSEED

Flaxseed is probably best known for assisting gut health. In short, this aperient plant helps the colon stay clean and effective by promoting healthy bowel movements. It's also known to lower blood pressure, improve cholesterol levels, stabilize blood sugar, and improve insulin resistance.[37] Other amazing benefits include menopause support, chronic fatigue, and improved skin conditions.[38] You can purchase flaxseed in whole or ground form, but you digest it better when it has been ground. Although delicious when added whole to baking, you'll want to use the ground form when adding it to smoothies.

Fun fact: Flaxseed also makes a great vegan egg! Simply combine one tablespoon of ground flaxseed with three tablespoons of water, stir well, and let sit for five minutes. Use this flax egg recipe to replace one traditional egg in baking recipes.

GARLIC

Botanically a root vegetable, garlic has been used for thousands of years as somewhat of a cure-all. Assisting with anything from fevers to stomach aches to diarrhea, garlic contains a multitude of health benefits. The root is used as a preventative medicine for cardiovascular disease and reduction of cancer risk, as well as for its antimicrobial and antioxidant effects.[39] Fresh garlic contains the most health benefits and is delicious when added to just about anything. My current favorite ways to consume this root is to roast it with other vegetables and drink it in a healing broth.

GINGER

Gingerroot is an absolute staple in our house. We use it for cooking, baking, and enhancing smoothies. Ginger can commonly be found fresh, crystalized, and dehydrated. It's often found in healthy juices, as well as in almost anything natural that's used for antinauseant purposes. When my children were young, ginger was what I reached for to reduce an upset tummy or motion sickness.

Aside from its antinausea effects, ginger is also effective in reducing inflammation, assisting with digestive issues, and reducing the risk of various metabolic syndromes. It's used to help soothe colds, migraines, joint pain, and hypertension.[40]

GINKGO

Ginkgo is widely known for its positive effects in prevention and treatment of cognition and age-related processes, but it also boasts a long list of other health benefits.[41] Clinical studies have shown that ginkgo's antiapoptotic, antioxidant, and anti-inflammatory properties can also help treat high blood pressure, cardiovascular disease, and insulin resistance.[42]

Found commonly in the forms of tablets, capsules, extracts, or tea, ginkgo makes an easy and healthful addition to a mid-morning or afternoon brain break.

GINSENG

Not unlike ginkgo, ginseng is an herb that has been widely studied for its incredible attributes surrounding treatment and prevention in neurodegenerative diseases, such as Parkinson's, Huntington's, and Alzheimer's.[43] It's been found to be cardioprotective, anticancer, and antihypertensive,[44] and has been proven to improve angina levels, as well as decrease cholesterol.[45]

Ginseng looks a little like gingerroot and can be consumed in the same ways. It can be eaten fresh or lightly cooked, brewed in teas, or taken in supplement form.

GRAPEFRUIT

This tangy citrus fruit provides more than its distinct, somewhat sour flavor. Grapefruit—especially the red and pink varieties—contain plenty of phytonutrients, including vitamins, minerals, antioxidants, carotenoids, and flavonoids. These little helpers assist to decrease inflammation in the body, reduce risk for cardiovascular disease, coronary heart disease, and ischemic stroke.[46] They help maintain a healthy body weight, and have beneficial effects on bone mineral content, blood lipids, and neuroinflammation.[47]

My favorite ways to consume grapefruit include juicing it, eating it fresh with a little stevia sprinkled on it, sipping a homemade grapefruit cooler on ice in the summer, and freezing it into ice cube trays for other fun summer drink ideas. There are no bad ideas when it comes to grapefruit.

Green Tea

Green tea (*Camellia sinensis*) has long been considered the superfood of Chinese medicine. The drink is teeming with vitamins, minerals, and antioxidants, and has a multitude of proven health benefits associated with it.

Peer-reviewed studies have shown that this functional beverage contributes to a reduction in the risk of certain types of cancer, cardiovascular disease, heart disease and liver disease.[48] It's prized for its role in the promotion of oral health and healthy body weight, and its physiological effects include being antihypertensive, antibacterial, and antiviral.[49] In addition, the drink offers neuroprotective power, solar ultraviolet protection, anti-fibrotic properties, and increased bone mineral density.[50] Green tea is a popular alternative to coffee, as it also contains caffeine but won't stain your teeth.

HIBISCUS

An incredibly fragrant flower that dries beautifully, hibiscus is a relatively common ingredient in cosmetics due to its dermatological benefits. Specifically, it protects our cells from collagen degradation, oxidative stress, and against the harmful effects of UV radiation.[51] Skin aside, the plant also helps to promote weight loss, reduce the growth of bacteria and cancer cells, and support the health of the heart and liver.[52] It's known to be anti-inflammatory, antioxidant, and antimicrobial.[53]

Also? It smells *amazing*.

Honey

Oh, honey. There are just so many impressive ways that this sweet syrup can help the human body. Friends, this is where I gush.

Clinical studies have shown honey to be effective as an anticancer agent. It minimizes and helps to prevent cell spread, modifies cell cycle progression, and initiates mitochondrial membrane depolarization.[54] This essentially means that honey can both prevent *and* reduce cancer cell growth. Other fun ways that honey assists the human body are equally as impressive. It positively modifies the immune response, and treats asthma, cough, fever, and inflammation.[55] Honey also helps reduce the risk for and treats gastrointestinal disease and neurological disorders.[56]

It's important to consume honey in the purest form possible to reap the most rewards. The less processed the better, and don't let raw unpasteurized honey scare you—this is a perfect food available exactly in the way nature intended.

Hops

Hops have been cultivated by humans for thousands of years.

Unfortunately, the most popular way in North America to consume hops is in beer, but supplements containing hops have been proven to be effective in the treatment of mild mood disorders.[57] A few specific ailments that this plant has shown effectiveness in treating include stress, anxiety, and depression.[58] Keep in mind that any benefits this herb offers is eradicated by ethanol's effects on your body. Sorry, folks—beer doesn't count.

Fresh or dried hops can be purchased online or at a local hop farm if you're close to one. They can be used to make a variety of healing drinks, including teas, tonics, and coolers.

KALE

Everyone knows (or should know by now) that kale is very good for you. Long touted as a superfood, this leafy green is absolutely teeming with phytochemicals, vitamins, minerals, and other good things—it is abundant in bioactive compounds! Kale is used globally in the prevention and treatment of chronic and degenerative diseases, including (but in no way limited to) high cholesterol levels, gastric ulcers, rheumatism, hyperglycemic, and hepatic diseases.[59] It boasts a much higher nutritional value when compared to other foods, and is grown easily anywhere due to its innate heartiness.

Kale can be easily used to make salads, soups, stews, smoothies, juices, and more. No excuses—everyone needs to make the effort to eat more of this incredible plant.

LAVENDER

This very fragrant plant is beautiful to view and smell and boasts some great health benefits. Studies have found lavender to be very effective in the reduction of anxiety and depression.[60] It also has many curative properties, from inducing relaxation to treating parasitic infections, insect bites, burns, and muscle spasms.[61]

Consuming lavender tea is a great way to wind down at the end of the day, and I personally also love dabbing some lavender essential oil on my wrists at bedtime. It pairs wonderfully with lemonade and makes delicious simple syrup for all kinds of healing drinks.

LEMON

Lemons are natural cleansers, and are rich in vitamins, minerals, essential oils, dietary fiber, and carotenoids.[62] The sour fruit is pleasant to smell and tangy to taste, and is a popular flavor for drinks, ice cream, sorbet, pie, and basically all the yummy things. Lemon may aid in weight loss and reduce your risk of heart disease, anemia, kidney stones, digestive issues, and cancer.[63] The fruit has a positive effect on lowering blood sugar and make fantastic cleaning agents due to their high acidity and antibacterial properties. It also offers alleviation for fatigue, as well as lipid-lowering effects.[64]

Lemons are used in a few different recipes within the book, including coolers, teas, smoothies, juices, and tonics.

LEMONGRASS

Lemongrass is a tropical plant native to the grass family. It's native to Africa, Asia, and Australia and is commonly found in Thai food. Only the bottom third of the stem is edible, as the top half can be barbed and very fibrous.

As its name suggests, this plant smells and tastes of lemon, but also sometimes ginger and even florals. Lemongrass is known to decrease blood pressure and improve overall cardiovascular health.[65]

MATCHA

Matcha is the powdered form of green tea containing very high amounts of antioxidant and anti-inflammatory compounds. It's been proven to have positive health-promoting effects on cardiovascular, metabolic, and cognitive function.[66] Matcha decreases stress and increases memory and attention.[67]

I've used matcha many ways, but my favorite ways include making matcha lattes and sprinkling the powder on baking and energy balls to take advantage of its appealing color. It also makes a fun and colorful addition to pancakes!

MISO

Miso is a fermented food made from soybeans. The microbial community of miso is thought to be crucial in enhancing its distinct flavor and texture as well as its nutritional properties. Its impressive nutrition profile contributes to its ability to prevent chronic disease and assist in gut health. It is known to be anticancer, antimicrobial, and anti-obesity, meaning that it assists in healthy weight maintenance.[68]

Miso broth is one of the healing recipes in this book, and the drink is teeming with healing and nutritive assets. It makes a wonderful alternative to bone broth for someone who is sick or healing from surgery but is not interested in consuming animal products.

MUSHROOM

Adaptogenic mushrooms (also called functional mushrooms or medicinal mushrooms) are different from the mushrooms we commonly find in the grocery store. These gems possess a strong and distinct set of healing abilities and are typically found to be antidiabetic, antioxidant, antimicrobial, anticancer, prebiotic, immunomodulating, and anti-inflammatory.[69] They also generally support the cardiovascular system and help with stress management, cognition, and energy.

Types of adaptogenic mushrooms include (but are not limited to) lion's mane, reishi, chaga, turkey tail, shitake, maitake, and cordyceps. They can be purchased at health food stores, online, and sometimes you can find them at Farmer's Markets or local herbal dispensaries. If you are into foraging, they can easily be found in the forests of the Pacific Northwest and are commonly made into healing drinks in the form of teas or broths.

Oat

I feel like oats (like all foods high in carbohydrates) get a bad rap these days. But oats are extremely healthy and boast an incredible nutrition profile that is full of fiber, protein, bioactive phytochemicals, and lots of other goodies.[70] They are rich in antioxidants and have a great amino acid balance. Oats give amazing immune system support and are anti-inflammatory, immunomodulatory, anticholesterolemic, antidiabetic, and help with wound healing.[71]

Oats can be mixed with plant-based mylk or water to create a traditional oatmeal. They can be added to baking, blended in smoothies, and made into flour. Oat mylk is super easy to make and one of my favorite plant-based mylks. If you're in the market for honest, quality oats, One Degree Organic Foods makes organic, sprouted, gluten-free, traceable products that boast some of the best quality oats I have ever come across—and they're sold in Costco all over North America, including Mexico.

How's that for healthfully accessible?!

ONION

In countless clinical reviews, authors cite an incredible number of benefits associated with onion consumption. They include (but are in no way limited to) anticarcinogenic properties, antiplatelet and antithrombic activity, and anti-asthmatic and antibiotic effects.[72] Onions are antimicrobial, antiviral, and contain a mixture of sulphureous compounds that contribute to antibacterial activity.

The second most popular horticultural crop after tomatoes, onions have been used for thousands of years in both preventative and curative ways. Onion broth is a nutritive and simple way to nourish, soothe, and repair, which is why it's one of the healing drinks featured in this book.

Orange

Oranges are part of the citrus family and are commonly known for their high levels of vitamin C. They are utilized for their energy, nutrients, and bioactivities, and have been helpful in developing new chemotherapeutic or complementary medicine in recent decades.[73] Specific characteristics of this yummy fruit include antioxidative, anti-inflammatory, anticancer, as well as cardiovascular protective effects, and neuroprotective effects.[74] Whole fruits (including peels) are known to treat high blood pressure, indigestion, cough, muscle pain, skin inflammation, and even ringworm infections.[75]

PARSLEY

This bright green herb is not just an attractive garnish found in restaurants! I don't know about you, but I cook with it all the time—and not just for the health benefits, of which it has plenty.

Hailing from the Mediterranean region, this highly medicinal plant possesses numerous benefits, including being antimicrobial, anti-anemic, anticoagulant, antihyperlipidemic, antihepatotoxic, antihypertensive, having diuretic effects, and having hypoglycemic, hypouricemic, anti-oxidative, and estrogenic activities.[76] Parsley is also used to treat certain health issues such as heavy menstrual bleeding, diabetes, arterial hypertension, and cardiac and renal diseases.[77] The herb can also be eaten to prevent and treat bloating, distention, and flatulence.[78]

PEPPERMINT

Peppermint tea is my absolute favorite, and I even enjoy it cold during the summer. It's refreshing, herbal, and freshens the breath. What's not to love?

Peppermint is fantastic for the gastrointestinal tract (it works particularly well for irritable bowel syndrome) and relaxes the central nervous system,[79] making it a great choice for winding down at the end of the day and after meals. The popular herb has shown significant antiviral and antimicrobial activities, strong antitumor and antioxidant actions, and even some antiallergenic potential.[80] It's also great for soothing headaches and general mild pain. It's also so easy to grow, dry, and preserve.

PINEAPPLE

This sweet and delicious fruit is always a hit (I have literally never met anybody who didn't like pineapple), but when you fully understand the positive health benefits of the wacky-looking fruit, you'll fall even more in love.

A rich source of vitamins and minerals, pineapple contains impressive amounts of bioactive compounds, dietary fiber, and other important nutrients. In addition, the fruit has been proven to be very anti-inflammatory, possess antioxidant activity, monitor nervous system function, and heal the bowel.[81]

You can eat pineapple on its own or add it to fruit salads. You can blend it in smoothies or freeze it and add it to drinks in the summertime. You can even bake with it, which is why pineapple upside-down cake is a thing. I've also used the hard core as a teething toy for my children when they were young. Simply freeze the core and offer to your teething babe between the ages of six and twelve months. (For more fun tips like this, check out my book titled *Baby Nosh!*)

ROSE

Rose and rose petal extract have been used for skincare for decades due to rose's high anti-inflammatory activity. The flower contains antioxidant and antimicrobial properties, which assist with skin inflammation of all kinds.[82] It's used as a common ingredient in face cream to reduce puffiness but can also be ingested (the herb, not the face cream). Rose-infused water provides anti-inflammatory hydration that assists the body from the inside out—but the benefits of rose are not limited to skincare.

The herb can be used for combatting depression, promoting psychological relaxation, improving sexual dysfunction, and for its powerful anti-anxiety effects.[83] Many people enjoy diffusing rose essential oils or sipping rose tea to reap the benefits of this lovely flower.

ROSEMARY

The therapeutic effects of rosemary are vast. This hearty, delicious, and very fragrant herb has traditionally been used as an antispasmodic (rosemary tea is great for a cough), mild analgesic, and to cure neuropathic chest pain. It's also used for headaches and migraines, and to treat insomnia, emotional upset, and depression.[84] The plant also shows positive clinical effects on learning, memory, mood, pain, anxiety, and sleep.[85]

The essential oil form of rosemary has been heavily researched with the intention to use it to help those suffering with varied nervous system disorders.[86] Rosemary has shown significant antimicrobial, anti-inflammatory, analgesic, antioxidant, anti-apoptotic, antitumor, antinociceptive, anticancer, and anticonvulsant activity.[87] It's also wound healing and has been used to treat infectious skin issues and promote hair and nail growth.[88]

THYME

Like rosemary, thyme is a fragrant and easily recognizable herb, used for culinary purposes as well as in functional medicine. Rich in vitamins A and C, thyme has therapeutic properties that include antioxidant, antiviral, antibacterial, antifungal, antiseptic, anti-inflammatory, and antineoplastic actions.[89] A medicinal gem of a plant, this herb can be found as a common ingredient in alternative medicine, as well as a natural preservative when added to food.[90]

In this book, I focus on thyme as a fantastic natural remedy for both cough and fungus.

TURMERIC

Turmeric is highly valued throughout the medical community, as it is an excellent source of polyphenol curcumin. It assists in the management of oxidative and inflammatory conditions, arthritis, anxiety, metabolic syndrome, and hyperlipidemia.[91] It also aids in the management of exercise-induced inflammation and muscle soreness, thus enhancing recovery and performance in those who lead active lifestyles.[92] Curcumin is also associated with the treatment of certain cancers by suppressing initiation, progression, and general metastasis of a variety of tumors,[93] making turmeric antimutative.

The orange-yellow root is commonly ingested in capsule form but is lovely when consumed as a warm drink or within cold-pressed juice. I love cozy turmeric tea or creamy steamed mylk, recipes for which can be found later in this book. The recipes within this book use turmeric in both powdered and root form. Roots are called "fingers," so a recipe might call for a one-inch portion of a turmeric finger. (I know—a portion of gingerroot is called a thumb. Someone had to make all this verbiage weird . . .)

Turmeric can stain your teeth when consumed often. I recommend following any turmeric drink up with a small glass of water, and then brushing your teeth—it's worth it. It also stains your fingers. Use gloves while handling it if an orange finger stain will bother you.

VANILLA

A primary component of this aromatic plant is called vanillin, which is known for its anticancer, antioxidant, anti-inflammatory, antifungal, antibiotic, antitumor, and anti-neuroinflammatory properties.[94] Vanilla is most often used for culinary ventures, but it has been shown to be beneficial in promoting healthy skin, hair, and oral health. Specifically, it treats acne, is anti-aging, soothes burns, and promotes hair growth.[95] Vanilla also acts as a menstrual and digestive aid and has wound healing properties.[96]

Turns out, vanilla is not so vanilla!

You can purchase vanilla easily in both extract and bean form. As with every other food you consume, try to purchase the purest form possible if procuring an extract.

WATERMELON

Watermelon is a summertime favorite and loved for its mild, sweet flavor and high water content. Watermelon can be considered an excellent functional food because of its rich lycopene, vitamins A and C content, antioxidant potentials, and bioactive compounds. It boasts numerous health benefits, including decreased risk of cardiovascular disease, age related ailments, obesity, diabetes, and various cancers. The yummy melon also contains properties helpful in alleviating ulcerative colitis.[97]

Feel free to eat to your heart's content when it comes to watermelon—there are too many health benefits to count.

Part Three: 50 Healing Drinks for 50 Common Afflictions

50 Afflictions

Different Types of Elixirs

This final part of the book—the lengthiest portion by far—is where we pair the fifty foods that we learned about in Part Two with fifty common health issues. From acne to weight management, this book provides an alphabetical list of general afflictions, healing foods to support the betterment of them, and associated recipes that I hope you will love as much as I do. Remember that although important in certain circumstances, we do not need to always rely on conventional medications to provide the relief we seek from our common complaints. Sometimes pharmaceuticals are very important and useful in the treatment of afflictions such as mood disorders and acute injuries, but most of the time? Clean, whole, living food is just *better*.

Every recipe in this book can be considered an elixir. Elixirs are intentional beverages concocted from ingredients that are meant to support various bodily functions and provide medicinal support to the person drinking them. In this section of the book, you'll find several different types of elixirs that fall under one of these seven definitions:

- **Broths:** warm, mostly clear drinks, rich in vitamins, minerals, and vegetable matter. Broths can be made in large batches and stored in the refrigerator for up to a week. They can also be poured into ice cube molds and frozen for later use. All broth recipes in this book make about four cups (thirty-two ounces) of broth.
- **Coolers:** filtered water infused with the essence of various botanicals. Coolers can be stored in a cool place for up to 3–4 days and are typically poured over ice for consumption. All cooler recipes in this book make about one to two cups (eight to sixteen ounces) of cooler.
- **Juices:** fresh-pressed juice using a hand or electric juicer. Typically, you want to juice the least juicy foods first, and the ones with the

most water content last. (For example, if ginger is in the recipe, it would almost always be juiced first. If cucumber is in the recipe, it would usually be juiced last.) Nutrients are extracted from their sources, leaving behind the fibrous parts of the plant. Juices can be stored in a cold environment for up to 3–4 days, though they're most nutritious if consumed immediately after juicing. All juice recipes in this book make about one cup (eight ounces) of fresh-pressed juice.

- **Mylks:** fresh and homemade plant-based milk alternatives that are often used as liquid portions of plant-based smoothies. Although best when fresh, mylks can be refrigerated and consumed within a few days to a week. All mylk recipes in this book make about two to three cups (sixteen to twenty-four ounces) of mylk.

- **Smoothies:** thick, blended drinks that are often used as meal replacements. Foods are blended intact, to retain the plants' fiber. Smoothies are best if consumed immediately after blending but can be frozen in ice cube trays to thaw and drink later. All smoothie recipes in this book make about one and a half to two cups (twelve to sixteen ounces) of smoothie.

- **Teas:** typically made with dried herbs (there are a few exceptions where the herbs may be fresh) and served hot as a medicinal remedy. Typically made at home on an as-needed basis. The usual dosage for tea is one tablespoon of dried herbs steeped in eight ounces of hot water. All tea recipes in this book make one cup (eight ounces) of tea.

- **Tonics:** solutions prepared from a select assortment of herbs; can be drunk either hot or cold. Tonics can often be found in hospitals, pharmacies, and food stores. They can be kept cold or at room temperature depending on the herbs used to prepare them. I advise consumption within 2–3 days to take full advantage of their medicinal properties. All tonic recipes in this book make about two to three cups (sixteen to twenty-four ounces) of tonic.

Healing Recipes

Acne (soothe)

Acne is an inflammatory disorder of the skin caused by plugged follicles. A mixture of oil and skin cells becomes trapped under the surface of the skin, which can produce pimples and even lesions. Acne can be painful and embarrassing and can cause permanent scarring if it's severe enough, so it's best to figure out what's causing it as quickly as possible (stress, diet, personal hygiene). People of all ages and ethnic backgrounds can be prone to acne, but it is most common among teenagers and young adults. This is one motivating reason to start incorporating healthy eating habits and learning about food's impact on your body at a young age.

There are several plants known to assist with skin health that, when combined with a preventative skin care routine, a healthy diet, and stress management, can help your skin stay clean, healthy, and glowing.

Helpful Foods
- Cashew
- Hibiscus
- Rose
- Vanilla

VANILLA CASHEW MYLK

Ingredients:
1 cup raw, unsalted cashews
3 cups filtered water
1 teaspoon pure vanilla extract
½ teaspoon cinnamon
1 teaspoon raw, unpasteurized honey or pure maple syrup (optional)

Method:
Soak cashews in water overnight (or for at least a few hours). Rinse and drain, then transfer to high-speed blender. Pour in filtered water, vanilla, cinnamon, and sweetener if you choose. Blend on high until smooth and creamy. Store in a sealed container for up to three days and shake well before drinking.

Tip: You can use this recipe for any other recipe that calls for cashew mylk as a single ingredient.

ANEMIA (STRENGTHEN)

Anemia is described as a reduction in the proportion of red blood cells, which are responsible for carrying oxygen and nutrients throughout the bloodstream. When these cells are depleted, the most common symptom is extreme fatigue. Other symptoms include shortness of breath, dizziness, or headaches.[1] Iron-deficiency anemia is often caused by recent menstruation and during pregnancy (which is why it's more common in women than men) and diets consistently low in heme iron (often a plant-based diet, since red meat is known to be the most bioavailable heme iron source).[2]

Although iron supplements are widely used for the treatment of anemia, they're not always as absorbable and successful as they claim to be, which has certainly been my own experience. This is where certain foods like beets come in. Beets are naturally high in iron, but the roots, stalks, and greens also stimulate the production of red blood cells, thereby increasing iron distribution throughout the body.[3] Remember: food is information, and your body needs to recognize it to use it well.

Helpful Foods
- Beet
- Carrot
- Kale

Fresh-Pressed Beet Juice

Ingredients:
1 thumb ginger
1 large carrot (with greens, if possible)
1 celery stalk with leaves
2 large beets with stalks and greens
1 medium apple
½ lemon

Method:
Clean all ingredients and chop beets and apple into quarters. Using your juicer, press all ingredients except lemon in the order listed above into a tall glass. Squeeze lemon over juice, and drink within 15 minutes.

Tip: If you're not a fan of the froth that will most likely be on top of the juice after juicing, simply scrape it off prior to consuming. Although full of nutrients, some people find their experience is better when the froth is removed.

Anxiety (soothe)

Anxiety is a very common feeling that people experience, some more often than others. It refers to anticipation of a future problem or concern and can be acute or chronic in nature. Anxiety is often met with physical symptoms like shallow breathing, muscle tension, and nausea. Emotionally, it is associated with (often) unfounded fears, avoidance behavior, and fight or flight reactions.[4]

Anxiety itself is not typically concerning, but how we deal with and react to it makes a huge difference in our experiences surrounding it. There are many helpful ways to lessen feelings of anxiety, including intentional deep breathing, exercise, meditation, and nutrition. Try the recipe for Lavender Lemon Cooler and see if you can stay as present as possible while sipping it. Make sure to smell, breathe deeply, and take a few minutes to notice the subtleties of the lavender in this delicious healing drink.

Helpful Foods
- Cacao
- Hops
- Lavender
- Rose
- Turmeric

Lavender Lemon Cooler

Ingredients:
2 sprigs fresh lavender
1 cup water
1 cup ice
½ lemon
Pinch stevia

Method:
Heat water in kettle to at least 85°F. Gently remove lavender buds from one sprig and add to the water, setting the second sprig aside. Cover and let steep for 10–15 minutes. Place ice in glass and then, using cheesecloth, strain hot lavender water into glass and over ice. Chop lemon into wedges and add to cooler. Add a pinch of stevia to taste, stir well, garnish with second lavender sprig, and enjoy.

Asthma (soothe, restore)

Asthma is a chronic condition that negatively affects the airways in the lungs. An immune response causes the airways to become inflamed and narrowed, making it harder for air to flow in and out.[5] This can make sufferers feel as though they can't breathe, which induces panic, which often makes the situation worse. Asthma can be triggered by food sensitivities, environmental conditions such as smoke, pollen, or mold, stress, infections, and physical activity.[6] There is also a spectrum of severity: some people experience mild asthma from time to time, while others must use a prescribed inhaler several times a day for their entire lives to breathe sufficiently.

The following foods have been shown to help reduce mild symptoms of asthma when consumed regularly, but they are in no way a replacement for medicine.[7] Severe asthma can be life-threatening and should be treated as such.

Helpful Foods
- Beet
- Garlic
- Ginseng
- Honey
- Lemon
- Peppermint
- Turmeric

Honey Ginseng Tea

Ingredients:
1 tablespoon dried ginseng
1 cup filtered water
¼ teaspoon raw, unpasteurized honey (optional)

Method:
Heat water in kettle to at least 85°F. Steep ginseng in water, covered, for 10–15 minutes. Remove herbs from water, stir in honey, and sip slowly.

BLOATING (SOOTHE, RESTORE)

Bloating and its twin sister distention are very common gastrointestinal complaints. They can be very uncomfortable and are symptoms of many different ailments. Whether you've eaten a large meal, consumed foods that you may be sensitive to (such as gluten or dairy), drank too many carbonated beverages, or are suffering from one or more of many common gastrointestinal afflictions, no one likes to feel bloated.

There are some ways to reduce bloating naturally, without grabbing an over-the-counter pharmaceutical that is often an inefficient bandage instead of a real solution. (We should be asking ourselves what caused the bloating in the first place and identifying ways to avoid it in the future.) Movement and exercise can be helpful, and abstaining from food for a few hours might do the trick. Following a low FODMAP diet is also known to assist those who find themselves suffering chronically from bloating.[8] One of my own tried-and-true methods I use to reduce unwanted feelings of fullness is to sip parsley tea.

Helpful Foods
- Flaxseed
- Parsley
- Watermelon

Parsley Tea

Ingredients:
1 tablespoon dried parsley
1 cup filtered water
¼ teaspoon raw, unpasteurized honey (optional)

Method:
Heat water in kettle to at least 85°F. Add parsley and steep covered for 10–15 minutes. Remove herbs from water, add honey if desired, and sip slowly.

Tip: Parsley is a hearty and easily grown herb. If you suffer from bloating regularly, consider planting some parsley in a garden or planter pot for quick and easy access.

Blood Pressure (strengthen, restore)

Blood pressure medication is one of the most common pharmaceuticals people in North America are prescribed, yet studies show that a diet overhaul can be just as effective—if not more—than commercial medications.[9] There are many plants listed in this book that assist with improving cardiovascular health, but a few that have been specifically proven to boast a multitude of hypotensive properties.

Helpful Foods
- Chamomile
- Ginkgo
- Ginseng
- Lemongrass
- Parsley

Lemongrass Tonic

Ingredients:
1 lemongrass stalk
1 small thumb ginger
4 cups filtered water
1 cup peppermint leaves
½ teaspoon stevia

Method:
Slice lemongrass stalk in half, then in half again lengthwise. Place in saucepan, along with peeled ginger. Add 4 cups cold water and bring to a boil over medium-high heat for 5 minutes. Add fresh mint and boil for 2 minutes or until fragrant. Remove from heat and, using a cheesecloth, strain tonic into a large jar or ceramic mug. Add stevia, stir, and enjoy.

Body Odor (restore)

While there are many foods that contribute to pungent body odor, there are also many with antibacterial properties that help to combat it. Most herbs are good at this job, and if you explore your local health food store's hygiene aisle, you're likely to find a handful of natural deodorants that feature essential oils and enzymes from the list you see below.

While topical deodorants obviously assist in masking odor, you can also ingest these plants orally to cultivate an internal environment that will support the issue of body odor from the inside out.

Helpful Foods
- Basil
- Blueberry
- Hops
- Lavender
- Lemon
- Lemongrass
- Rosemary
- Sage

BASIL BLUEBERRY COOLER

Ingredients:
½ cup blueberries
6 basil leaves
1 cup ice
1 cup water
Pinch stevia

Method:
Clean basil and blueberries. Rub basil between fingers to release more flavor. Place ice in glass, then add plants. Add cold water and stevia if desired. Stir well, sip, and enjoy.

Tip: Smash blueberries for increased absorption or eat them whole after drinking the cooler.

BRUISING (SOOTHE, RESTORE)

A bruise is a very common skin injury that results in a collection of blood near the surface of the skin. This produces a black or blue appearance at first that gradually settles into yellow and sometimes green tones before eventually disappearing. Bruising can last from days to weeks depending on the severity of the injury. There is usually some pain at the bruise site at first, but this typically goes away before the bruise does. In any case, bruises tend to be unsightly, and their lifespan can be reduced by ingesting certain plants and herbs.

Helpful Foods
- Aloe
- Chamomile
- Kale
- Lemon
- Orange
- Parsley
- Pineapple

Citrus Chamomile Tea

Ingredients:
1 tablespoon dried chamomile
1 orange wedge
1 lemon wedge
1 cup filtered water

Method:
Heat water in kettle to at least 85°F. Add dried herbs and steep, covered, for 10–15 minutes. Remove chamomile from water, pour into a mug, squeeze juice from citrus wedges over top of the tea, and enjoy.

Cold and Flu (soothe)

When it comes to cold and flu, the variety of symptoms can be both scattered and plentiful: aches, pain, chills, fever, headaches, lethargy, reduced appetite, nausea, and more. Clinical studies have shown that vitamin C helps to shorten the duration of these symptoms when you contract a cold or flu—but it works the best when taken preventatively.[10] Instead of taking daily vitamin C supplements, why not go straight to the source?

Citrus contains naturally high levels of this wonder vitamin, so drinking a glass of citrus water once per day during cold and flu season could help you reduce the amount and duration of symptoms you'll feel when you do catch that inevitable winter virus. Plus, water helps with hydration, which is always a good thing.

Helpful Foods
- Grapefruit
- Lemon
- Orange

Rainbow Citrus Cooler

Ingredients:
1 lemon slice
1 orange slice
1 grapefruit slice
1 lime slice
½ cup ice
1 cup water

Method:
Clean and slice your citrus (the rind goes in the glass, so cleaning it first is recommended). Place ice in glass. Squeeze each citrus slice or wedge softly over ice before adding fruit to glass. Add cold water, stir well, sip, and enjoy.

Tip: although the recipe makes about 10 ounces of liquid, use a large glass to account for the ice and fruit. You can also make a whole pitcher of this drink and keep it in your fridge for up to three days for easy grab-and-go.

Constipation (restore)

Constipation occurs when bowel movements become less frequent and stools become difficult (and in some cases painful) to pass. This typically happens when there is not enough fiber in your diet, or you've eaten something that your body is sensitive to (such as dairy). It can also be the result of medication, or simply not enough activity.

A plant-based diet is the most amazing thing for preventing constipation, as plants are full of both soluble and insoluble fiber, hydrating because of their inherent water content, and naturally quick to digest. Extra water also helps, along with the plants associated with this recipe.

Helpful Foods
- Aloe
- Blueberry
- Flaxseed
- Kale

Blueberry Flaxseed Smoothie

Ingredients:
1 cup unsweetened almond mylk
½ cup frozen blueberries
½ banana, peeled
2 tablespoons ground flaxseed
½ cup ice

Method:
Add all ingredients to blender and blend until smooth. Enjoy immediately, as flaxseed will thicken and become gelatinous if not consumed right away.

Cough (soothe)

Coughing is an important reflex that helps protect your airway and lungs against irritants. Occasional coughing is normal, because that's how your body clears your throat of germs, dust, and unwanted mucus. However, when coughing is persistent and becomes painful, that's when we can all agree that enough is enough. Although we rarely want to stifle a cough (our airways are protesting for a reason), there are ways to make healing drinks that will assist with lasting cough and the pain associated with it.

Aside from the tried-and-true lemon with honey recipe that most of us are familiar with, I recommend trying the following recipe for Lavender Hibiscus Tea.

Helpful Foods
- Fennel
- Hibiscus
- Honey
- Lavender
- Lemon
- Thyme

Lavender Hibiscus Tea

Ingredients:
½ tablespoon dried lavender
½ tablespoon dried hibiscus
1 cup filtered water
Raw, unpasteurized honey to taste (optional)

Method:
Heat water in kettle to at least 85°F. Combine dried herbs with hot water and steep, covered, for 10–15 minutes. Remove herbs from water, add honey if desired, and sip slowly.

Dehydration (restore)

Most people don't drink enough water. Our bodies are made of mostly water, so not only is it important to drink enough to replace what's lost during urination and perspiration, it's also important for detoxification and basic cellular growth and repair.[11]

From an athletic standpoint, conventional electrolyte drinks are often full of synthetic ingredients and very high in sugar. I always tell my kids that unsweetened coconut water (which is naturally sweet!) is the ultimate sports drink, because it's full of natural electrolytes, which are necessary for basic life functioning, balancing, and growth. If you've never made your own coconut water, you're in for a treat. Fresh coconut water is incredibly delicious, extremely hydrating, and contains the necessary components for cellular repair.

Helpful Foods
- Coconut
- Cucumber
- Watermelon

Pure Coconut Cooler

Ingredients:
Water from 1 coconut
Meat from ½ coconut (about ½ cup)
½ cup filtered water
1 cup ice

Method:
Crack open the coconut using the blunt end of something strong. (I prefer to use a hammer; my husband likes to use a drill.) Pour water straight from the coconut into a blender. Then, using a strong knife, peel away the brown coconut casing until the white coconut meat is exposed. Cut or scrape the coconut meat into pieces until you have enough to fill about half a cup. Place the coconut meat into the blender, add the filtered water, and blend. Place ice in large glass and pour blended coconut water from blender over top. Enjoy!

Tip: If you don't like the coconut pulp, strain liquid to capture and remove prior to drinking.

Depression (soothe, restore)

The American Psychiatric Association defines depression as "a mood disorder that causes a persistent feeling of sadness and loss of interest" and common symptoms of depression include "sadness, emptiness, or irritable mood, accompanied by somatic and cognitive changes that significantly affect the individual's capacity to function."[12]

Mood fluctuations plague most of us from time to time, but depression can be serious and even life-threatening. You'll remember from the introduction to Part Three of this book that I wrote about how pharmaceuticals can be very important and helpful for some of the ailments listed in this book—and this is one of them. Aside from medication, healthy food, exercise, and mindfulness are all ways to support recovery from depression. The following plants are known to assist with mood disorders and can be a welcome supplement to any wellness plan you may be following.

Helpful Foods
- Cacao
- Hops
- Lavender
- Rose
- Rosemary

Nut Butter Cacao Smoothie

Ingredients:
1 ripe banana
1 tablespoon cacao powder
1 tablespoon unsweetened nut butter
¼ cup oats
1 cup unsweetened almond mylk
½ cup ice

Method:
Add all ingredients to blender and blend until smooth. Pour into large glass and enjoy! This smoothie could honestly be a dessert, it's so good.

Detoxification (strengthen, restore)

Our body detoxifies itself in many ways, through perspiration, urination, defecation, and via multiple organ systems and processes. Lemons are fantastic agents of detoxification due to their high acidity and antibacterial properties. They promote better digestion by cleansing the gut, which in turn helps to detoxify the entire gastrointestinal system. The fruit also offers protective effects for the liver and kidneys, which allows for those organs to do their jobs more efficiently and effectively. Drinking lemon water also promotes hydration, which assists in healthy perspiration of the skin.

Helpful Foods
- Cayenne
- Dandelion
- Echinacea
- Garlic
- Ginger
- Ginseng
- Green tea
- Hibiscus
- Lemon
- Rosemary
- Thyme
- Turmeric

LEMON TONIC

Ingredients:
2 lemons
3 cups filtered water

Method:
Wash lemons. Slice, then place the entire fruit into a large glass. Fill with filtered water and immerse for at least 30 minutes on the counter. Add ice if desired and sip.

Tip: To make this simple drink more complex, try squeezing lemon into prepared Green Tea instead of water, or adding some hibiscus or ginger to this recipe.

Diabetes (strengthen, restore)

Diabetes is a condition in which the body doesn't produce enough insulin or can't use it as well as it should. When there isn't enough insulin, or cells stop responding to the insulin your body does produce, too much blood sugar stays in your bloodstream. Eventually, this can cause a variety of serious health issues.

Like most afflictions, food plays a vital role in diabetes prevention and to some extent treatment. By consuming a relatively sugar-free diet, limiting alcohol consumption, eating at regular intervals, exercising consistently, and monitoring your weight, you can greatly reduce your risk of developing diabetes or its precursor, insulin resistance.[13]

Helpful Foods
- Almond
- Beet
- Blueberry
- Cinnamon
- Coconut
- Flaxseed
- Kale
- Lemon
- Oat
- Onion
- Parsley
- Turmeric

Metabolic Tonic

Ingredients:
1 tablespoon olive oil
1 large yellow onion, chopped
2 cloves garlic, minced
2 tablespoons fresh thyme, chopped
4 cups vegetable broth
1 tablespoon fresh parsley, chopped

Method:
Add oil to a medium-sized pot and heat until warm. Add onion, garlic, and thyme to pan and let simmer on low until onions caramelize or turn slightly golden. Add vegetable broth and stir. Slowly cook until onions are transparent, then remove from heat. Ladle broth into a bowl or mug, sprinkle with fresh parsley, and enjoy.

Eyesight (strengthen)

Eye health is often put on the back burner, but this is a mistake. Aside from receiving annual eye exams that can help detect ocular disease, you can also preventatively treat your eyes to plants that have the power to strengthen them. The following plants are in this book's list of fifty and are very easy to incorporate into your weekly nutrition regimen. Whether you juice these ingredients, cook with them, consume them raw, or brew them into tea (okay, maybe not carrot!), they all make excellent nutritive eyesight supplements.

Helpful Foods
- Carrot
- Fennel
- Ginkgo
- Turmeric

Fresh-Pressed Carrot Juice

Ingredients:
1 thumb ginger
1-inch portion turmeric finger
4 large carrots
1 apple

Method:
Remove skin from ginger and turmeric. Clean carrots and apple and chop them into quarters. Using your juicer, press ginger, turmeric, carrots, then apple into a tall glass in that order. Drink within 15 minutes.

Tips: Follow up this recipe with a glass of water, then brush your teeth to prevent the staining effects of the turmeric. Also, I encourage you to juice the carrots unpeeled. The peels contain nutrients, and you won't even know they were there once they've been juiced.

Fatigue (restore)

Unwanted and persistent fatigue can be awful, and it doesn't discriminate. It's a common complaint among people of all ages, genders, and ethnic backgrounds. It plagues us all from time to time, and not surprisingly, the go-to drink to combat it is coffee (official drink of shift workers and busy parents *everywhere*).

The caffeine naturally found in coffee has been shown time and again in various clinical studies to assist with fatigue and overall exhaustion.[14] Since almonds are proven to enhance cognitive performance,[15] a coffee prepared with almond mylk is the perfect way to boost energy and help you stay alert for longer.

Helpful Foods
- Almonds
- Coffee
- Ginseng
- Green tea

Almond Mylk Espresso Affogato

Ingredients:
½ cup ice
1–2 ounces espresso (depending on the strength you prefer your coffee)
1½ cups unsweetened almond mylk
Raw honey or stevia (optional)

Method:
Place ice in a tall glass. Brew espresso and pour over ice. Slowly add almond mylk, lightly stir, and enjoy! If you prefer to sweeten this drink, try a touch of raw honey or a pinch of stevia.

Focus (restore)

With so much distraction in our modern lives filled with technology at our fingertips, it's no wonder people are having a difficult time focusing. It's important to note that there is a very large difference between lack of focus and attention deficit disorders. For this recipe, we are focusing (see what I did there?) on general lack of focus and not a clinically diagnosed disorder that I want to be careful not to underestimate or undermine.

There are several helpful foods whose unique compounds can contribute to heightened levels of cognition, and two are featured in the following recipe: oats and matcha.

Helpful Foods
- Coffee
- Ginkgo
- Ginseng
- Green tea
- Matcha
- Oat

Matcha Oat Mylk Latte, Two Ways

Ingredients:
1½ cups oat mylk
1½ teaspoons matcha powder
1½ tablespoons raw, unpasteurized honey

Method:
Way One (using a frother): Combine matcha with a touch of hot water in a mug and stir until it becomes a paste. Heat the oat mylk and froth until foamy. Pour over matcha. Add honey, mix well, and enjoy.

Way Two (using a stove): Simply combine all three ingredients in a small pot on the stove. Slowly heat on medium and whisk periodically until ingredients are well combined and hot, but not yet simmering. Once you are satisfied with the temperature and consistency, pour into your favorite mug, and enjoy.

Fungus (soothe, restore)

Many fungi live naturally in our mouths, gastrointestinal tracts, and skin, but can quickly overgrow under certain circumstances. When this overgrowth occurs, the result can produce a fungal infection. Fungal infections are most common on your skin and nails, but these infections can also cause issues in your mouth, throat, lungs, urinary tract, genitals, and many other parts of your body.

There are several plants that are considered antifungal, including the ones listed below. When we consume them, they can assist with lessening or stopping the growth of yeasts or molds that may be present and overgrowing.

Helpful Foods
- Aloe
- Blueberry
- Cayenne
- Garlic
- Lemon
- Onion
- Peppermint
- Rosemary
- Thyme
- Turmeric

BLUEBERRY THYME COOLER

Ingredients:
½ cup blueberries
Few sprigs of fresh thyme
1 cup ice
1 cup water
Pinch stevia

Method:
Clean your thyme and blueberries. Rub thyme between fingers to release more flavor. Place ice in glass, then add plants. Add cold water and stevia if desired. Stir well, sip, and enjoy.

Tip: For topical fungus treatment, oregano oil is by far the most effective. Once you make peace with its strong odor, you'll want to permanently add it to your basket of medicinal cures. Oregano oil can also be ingested in very small quantities, but as with all essential oils, be sure to procure ones that are safe and created specifically for ingestion.

Gut Health
(soothe, strengthen, restore)

When it comes to gut health and healing your digestive tract, the answer usually has something to do with balancing gut flora. Our digestive tracts are full of both good and bad bacteria, and when the balance is off, the entire body is typically affected. Eating foods that contain beneficial bacteria is crucial, which is why miso is the star of the following recipe for good gut health.

The fermentation process involved in the production of miso promotes levels of probiotics.[16] Other fermented foods like sauerkraut, good quality yogurts, kefir, and kombucha (both of which are mentioned in Part One of this book) are also excellent for gut health.

Helpful Foods
- Almond
- Avocado
- Flaxseed
- Miso

Traditional Miso Broth

Ingredients:
4 cups vegetable broth
3 tablespoons organic miso paste
¼ cup green onion, chopped
¼ cup organic firm tofu, pressed and cubed

Method:
Place miso paste into a small bowl, add a little hot water, and whisk until smooth. Set aside. Place broth in a medium saucepan and bring to a low simmer. Add green onion and tofu. Cook for 5–7 minutes. Remove from heat, add miso paste, and stir to combine well. Enjoy warm.

Tip: Adjust the amount of miso paste you use according to how strong you want the flavor to be. You also may want to adjust the amount of green onion and/or tofu you use according to your personal preference.

Hair and Nails (strengthen)

Supporting healthy hair and nails can be done easily and inexpensively with food. There is a plethora of products out there that claim to work miracles on hair and nails, but most of the time, these heavily marketed cosmetics are full of filler, synthetic chemicals, and toxic ingredients—and they're expensive.

The following foods are clinically proven to contain compounds that support hair and nails, naturally. These beautiful plants are plentiful, tasty, and really do work magic on your entire body—and they do it for a fraction of the cost of the commercially marketed stuff.

Helpful Foods
- Aloe
- Chamomile
- Dandelion
- Green tea
- Hibiscus
- Peppermint
- Rose
- Rosemary
- Turmeric

Rosemary Tea

Ingredients:
1 tablespoon dried rosemary
1 teaspoon pure maple syrup
1 cup filtered water

Method:
Boil water in kettle to at least 85°F. Add rosemary to water and steep, covered, for at least 15 minutes. Remove herbs and pour into your favorite mug. Add maple syrup and enjoy the tea warm or at room temperature.

Halitosis (restore)

Halitosis is a pretty term for bad breath. It's caused by bacteria that can grow in your mouth due to a variety of reasons including poor oral hygiene, an infected tooth or abscess, and oral yeast infections.[17] Knowing why you have bad breath is important because eliminating the root cause can encourage its departure, but the associated healing recipe is also helpful.

Helpful Foods
- Basil
- Fennel
- Parsley
- Peppermint
- Rosemary

HERB + GARDEN COOLER

Ingredients:
¼ cup fresh parsley, chopped
¼ cup fresh basil, chopped
1 rosemary twig
2 cups filtered water
1 fennel frond
1 cup ice (optional)

Method:
Wash herbs. Add parsley, basil, and rosemary to a large glass or jar. Fill with filtered water and swirl with fennel frond to mix well. Let sit for 10–15 minutes to allow herbs to fully infuse, then strain herbs from water. Add ice to infused water if desired and sip that bad breath away!

Tip: Eating the strained parsley and basil will also help eliminate bad breath. Just be sure to brush your teeth after!

HANGOVER (SOOTHE, RESTORE)

No one really intends to drink too much alcohol, but sometimes it happens. When it does, the result is usually a hangover. Hangovers are different for everyone and range from mild headache and tiredness to extreme nausea and vomiting. Other symptoms of hangover include tremulousness, diarrhea, and decreased cognitive or visual-spatial performance.[18] These symptoms are caused by dehydration, hormonal alterations, and the toxic and poisonous effects of the alcohol itself.

The following plants contain compounds that are known to help alleviate various symptoms of hangover.

Helpful Foods
- Ginger
- Ginseng
- Lemon
- Peppermint

Lemon Ginger Tea

Ingredients:
1 small thumb ginger
½ lemon
1 cup filtered water

Method:
Heat water in kettle to at least 85°F. Chop ginger and drop in water. Steep, covered, for 10–15 minutes. Remove ginger from water, squeeze lemon over top, and sip slowly.

Tip: Drinking this concoction *before* you consume alcohol can also help with the impending hangover. Coconut water is also a good preventive healing drink for this.

Hay Fever (soothe, restore)

Hay fever refers to seasonal allergies. It can cause cold-like symptoms, such as a runny nose, itchy eyes or throat, cough, watery eyes, congestion, sneezing, and general sinus pressure. While there are many pharmaceuticals dedicated to lessening the symptoms of hay fever, there are natural remedies that will also work like a charm without the drowsy side effects.

Two of the foods listed in this book are highly praised for their roles in assisting with hay fever symptoms: aloe and honey. (The rest on this list are pretty awesome, too.)

Helpful Foods
- Aloe
- Ginger
- Grapefruit
- Honey
- Lemon
- Onion
- Orange
- Turmeric

HONEY GINGER COOLER

Ingredients:
1 small thumb ginger
3 tablespoons aloe
1 tablespoon raw, unpasteurized honey
2 cups filtered water
Ice

Method:
Combine all ingredients in blender and blend until mixed well. Sip on an empty stomach, first thing in the morning. Repeat each day throughout allergy season.

Tip: The aloe in this healing drink is also fantastic for gut health.

Headaches (soothe)

Headaches can be caused by a multitude of triggers: cold and flu, sinus infection, tense neck and shoulder muscles, loud noises, premenstrual syndrome, injury, eyestrain, seasonal allergies, and more. Some headaches are quite mild and short in duration, while others evolve into migraines that can last days. Whatever your reason for a headache, it's always best to try to ward it off while it's on the mild side and close to the onset.

Helpful Foods
- Coffee
- Ginger
- Lavender
- Peppermint
- Rosemary

CLASSIC PEPPERMINT TEA

Ingredients:
1 tablespoon dried peppermint
1 cup filtered water
¼ teaspoon raw, unpasteurized honey (optional)

Method:
Heat water in kettle to at least 85°F. Steep dried peppermint in water, covered, for 10–15 minutes. Remove herbs from water, add honey if desired, and sip slowly.

Tip: If you love this tea as much as I do, try doubling the peppermint. (I often drink this tea at double strength.)

Heartburn (soothe, restore)

Heartburn is also called acid reflux, which is a common disorder characterized by symptoms associated with increased stomach acid exposure to the throat.[19] This condition is very common for overweight and pregnant women to experience (especially in the third trimester), but it also regularly affects people who consume diets high in sugar, fat, fried foods, alcohol, caffeine, and carbonated beverages.[20]

The key to finding functional foods that assist with heartburn lies in the foods' containment of acid-suppressive and anti-inflammatory agents—which the foods associated with this affliction all possess.

Helpful Foods
- Almond
- Blueberry
- Carrot
- Cashew
- Celery
- Cucumber
- Fennel
- Ginger
- Honey
- Kale
- Oats
- Watermelon

Reduce Juice

Ingredients:
1 large thumb ginger
2 large carrots
2 kale leaves
2 celery stalks
1 cucumber

Method:
Clean all ingredients. Using your juicer, press all ingredients in the order listed above. Sip slowly and enjoy.

Heart Health (strengthen)

Heart healthy living involves making positive lifestyle choices that contribute to a strong cardiovascular system. This means lots of mobility, challenging your fitness level regularly, making healthy food choices, and actively participating in stress-reducing activities, such as practicing mindfulness and intentional breath.

As far as food goes, plants are the answer (as always). The specific plants listed in this section are known for supporting cardiovascular health.

Helpful Foods
- Almond
- Avocado
- Blueberry
- Cashew
- Celery
- Garlic
- Ginkgo
- Grapefruit
- Green tea
- Lemongrass
- Matcha
- Mushroom
- Orange
- Watermelon

Big Green Smoothie

Ingredients:
1 kiwi
1 orange
1 cup kale
½ avocado
4–5 peppermint leaves
½ cup water
Handful of ice cubes

Method:
Peel the orange and kiwi. Combine all ingredients into blender and blend until smooth. Enjoy while cold.

Tip: If it doesn't freak you out, blend the kiwi intact. This fruit's fuzzy peel contains a lot of goodness and doesn't really taste like anything at all.

IMMUNITY (STRENGTHEN, RESTORE)

Your immune system plays an important role in keeping you alive. Its primary function is to prevent and clear infection, so we should always take care to make sure it's running smoothly.[21] Since the gut microbiome affects immunity to a larger extent than we've realized in the past, it's imperative that we eat foods to support it, as well as consume foods that support our immune system directly—so let's talk about vitamin C.

Vitamin C is an essential micronutrient that helps to support the immune system. In a recent study on the topic of vitamin C's role in a healthy immune system, authors explain: "Vitamin C contributes to immune defense by supporting various cellular functions of both the innate and adaptive immune system. Vitamin C supports epithelial barrier function against pathogens and promotes the oxidant scavenging activity of the skin, thereby potentially protecting against environmental oxidative stress."[22] Foods high in vitamin C include (but are not limited to) the members of the citrus family.

Another plant-based food that has a significant impact on immunity is oat. Oats contain copper, iron, selenium, and zinc, which help optimize the immune system in response to infection.[23]

Helpful Foods
- Carrot
- Ginger
- Grapefruit
- Lemon
- Oat
- Orange

Citrus Ginger Smoothie

Ingredients:
½ cup pineapple, peeled and chopped
½ orange, peeled
Small thumb of ginger, peeled and chopped
½ cup unsweetened oat mylk
½ cup ice
¼ lemon

Method:
Place all ingredients except lemon in blender and blend until smooth. Pour into glass and squeeze lemon wedge over top, being careful to not let any rogue seeds fall into the drink. Enjoy immediately.

Tip: This recipe makes excellent popsicles. Freeze into reusable popsicle molds for a healing summertime snack.

Inflammation (soothe, restore)

Inflammation is part of the body's amazing defense system. It is the process in which the immune system recognizes and removes harmful and foreign matter and drives the healing process. Inflammation is designed to be a good thing, but chronic inflammation can create more problems than solutions. There are many different reasons for chronic inflammation, which include (but are not limited to) autoimmune disorders, exposure to toxins, infection, stress, injury, regular alcohol composition, and obesity.[24]

A very good way to help your body reduce unwanted or unnecessary inflammation is by taking firm control of your diet. By choosing to consume plants that soothe and restore, we can make a huge difference to the amount of chronic inflammation that lives within our bodies. The following list of foods represent just over half of the plants featured in this book, and it is no mistake that so many fall into the anti-inflammatory category.

Helpful Foods

- Aloe
- Avocado
- Chamomile
- Chlorophyll
- Cinnamon
- Cucumber
- Dandelion
- Echinacea
- Fennel
- Garlic
- Ginger
- Ginkgo
- Ginseng
- Green tea
- Hibiscus
- Honey
- Matcha
- Mushroom
- Oat
- Orange
- Peppermint
- Pineapple
- Rose
- Rosemary
- Thyme
- Turmeric
- Vanilla

Cucumber Mint Cooler

Ingredients:
1 small bunch peppermint
1 cucumber
½ cup ice
½ cup filtered water
1 teaspoon liquid unflavored chlorophyll
Pinch stevia

Method:
Place mint, cucumber, and ice in glass. Add water, chlorophyll, and stevia. Stir well, sip, and enjoy.

Tip: For better infusion, try juicing the mint and cucumber (in that order) before adding to glass.

INSOMNIA (RESTORE)

As someone who has experienced bouts of insomnia, I can tell you the inability to sleep when you are tired is beyond brutal. Sleep is so incredibly necessary for our bodies to grow and repair tissue, heal from illness and injury, and consolidate mental and emotional processes and challenges. When you can't sleep, your body can't do any of these things and you feel those effects immediately.

Enter lovely lavender. The many positive effects that lavender has on the body are simply incredible. In countless clinical studies, this floral has been proven to improve functions of the nervous system that directly impact not only sleep, but also anxiety, depression, and pain.[25]

Helpful Foods
- Aloe
- Chamomile
- Hibiscus
- Hops
- Lavender

Calming Lavender Tea

Ingredients:
1 tablespoon dried lavender buds
1 cup filtered water
¼ teaspoon raw, unpasteurized honey (optional)

Method:
Heat water in kettle to at least 85°F. Steep lavender buds in water, covered, for 10–15 minutes. Remove herbs from water, add honey if desired, and sip slowly.

Tip: Lavender can be clipped in the summer, and if dried properly, maintain its shape, color, and fragrance for months. If you ever find yourself in a lavender field, be sure to set a few hours aside to prepare and dry a bundle of this floral. You'll thank yourself for it come winter.

Insulin Resistance (restore)

Insulin resistance is when the cells in your body don't respond well to insulin and can't easily take up glucose from your blood. In turn, your pancreas works harder to create more insulin to help glucose enter your cells.[26] The result is too much insulin in your body, which leads to a whole host of unwanted symptoms including fat accumulation and weight gain.

The term "prediabetes" is often used in conjunction with insulin resistance—it's a precursor to developing type 2 diabetes and should be taken seriously to avoid a future diabetes diagnosis. Consuming foods that regulate blood sugar, are high in fiber, and are low on the glycemic index can be very helpful in combatting this affliction.[27]

Helpful Foods
- Almond
- Beet
- Blueberry
- Cacao
- Cinnamon
- Coconut
- Flaxseed
- Kale
- Lemon
- Oat
- Onion
- Parsley
- Turmeric

Classic Cinnamon Oat Mylk

Ingredients:
1 cup whole oats (oat groats)
3 cups filtered water
1 teaspoon cinnamon
1 tablespoon maple syrup (optional)

Method:
Soak oats in 3 cups water overnight (or for at least a few hours). Place in high-speed blender with cinnamon and maple syrup if you choose. Blend on high until smooth. Using a cheesecloth, drain mylk into a bowl, then transfer to a sealed container for up to three days. Shake well before drinking, as separation will likely occur.

Tips: Swap pure maple syrup for raw and unpasteurized honey if you desire. To increase the bioavailability of the oats and make your drink more digestible, try using oats that are sprouted. (My favorite sprouted oat brand is One Degree Organics.)

Joint Pain (soothe)

Joint pain can be felt throughout your body, and when felt chronically, is usually a symptom of many different health conditions. Arthritis is the most common cause of joint pain, and there are dozens of different types. Joint pain may range from mild to severe, and treatments can vary from medicinal home care to surgery depending on the severity of your condition.

Some of the ways we can help alleviate joint pain include regular movement, lots of hydration, and consuming plants known to be effective in reducing inflammation within the body. Plants that are known to assist with the alleviation of joint pain are known as antirheumatic.

Helpful Foods
- Ginger
- Ginseng
- Turmeric
- Watermelon

Frozen Watermelon Cooler

Ingredients:
1 cup fresh watermelon, cubed
1 cup ice
Thyme or rosemary for garnish (optional)

Method:
Combine watermelon and ice in blender and blend until smooth. Pour in tall glass, garnish with thyme or rosemary, and drink immediately.

Tip: If you're feeling brave (as you may have mixed feelings about the combination of ginger and watermelon), try adding a very small amount of grated ginger to this cooler, as ginger is very good for alleviating inflammation leading to joint pain. I find it oddly goes well with watermelon.

Kidney Health (strengthen, restore)

Think of your kidneys as the ultimate filtration system for your body. They remove waste products from the blood and produce urine to assist with detoxification and to rid our bodies of excess fluid. Kidneys also help to maintain healthy levels of water, salt, and minerals.[28] Our kidneys are important, so let's give them some love by providing our bodies with foods known to support them!

Helpful Foods
- Blueberry
- Cranberry
- Garlic
- Ginger
- Onion
- Pineapple
- Turmeric

PULPY PINEAPPLE GINGER COOLER

Ingredients:
1 cup fresh pineapple
1 small thumb ginger, peeled
½ teaspoon powdered turmeric
1 cup filtered water
½ cup ice

Method:
Place pineapple, ginger, turmeric, and water in blender and blend until smooth. Add ice to tall glass, pour blend over ice, and enjoy.

Lactation (strengthen)

You may have heard that drinking beer might help new mothers lactate, but it's the hops in beer—not the beer itself—that has been shown to promote lactation. Consuming alcohol is not something anyone should recommend for breastfeeding mothers.

Hops contain galactagogues, which purportedly help increase the flow of a mother's breastmilk. There is conflicting evidence on this, but some studies have shown hops to have a very positive influence on milk production.[29] Hops tea is typically available in health food stores, though it's easy enough to make your own.

Helpful Foods
- Chamomile
- Cinnamon
- Fennel
- Garlic
- Hops
- Parsley
- Peppermint
- Rosemary
- Thyme

Calming Hops Tea

Ingredients:
1 tablespoon dried hops
2 cinnamon sticks
1 cup filtered water

Method:
Heat water in kettle to at least 85°F. Combine crushed hops and cinnamon in water and steep, covered, for 10–15 minutes. Remove hops and cinnamon sticks, stir, pour into your favorite mug, and enjoy. (You may also choose to keep a cinnamon stick in your tea while you sip—the smell is heavenly, and the cinnamon is warming.)

Tip: Fresh hops cones are harvested in the late summer, so be sure to stock up before September. Once properly dried, they can last until the following hops season commences.

Liver Health (strengthen)

Your liver is an essential organ whose task is to rid your body of toxic substances and old red blood cells, make bile used to break down food, metabolize macronutrients, produce substances required for blood clotting, regulate blood volume in the body, and store vitamins so the body can use them later.[30] It's very resilient and capable of regenerating itself by growing new cells to replace ones that die prematurely due to even minimal drugs and alcohol use. But if you abuse your liver for long enough, this important organ will become unhealthy, and this will greatly impact your overall health.

By preventatively and consistently treating your liver to a little love by providing it with functional foods to help it thrive, you positively support your whole entire body.

Helpful Foods

- Almond
- Beet
- Blueberry
- Cashew
- Coffee
- Cranberry
- Dandelion
- Grapefruit
- Green tea
- Kale
- Mushroom
- Parsley
- Rosemary
- Turmeric

MIXED ADAPTOGENIC MUSHROOM BROTH

Ingredients:
4 cups water
2 stalks celery, chopped
2 large carrots, chopped
2 cloves of garlic, minced
2 thumbs ginger, minced
1 yellow onion, chopped
1 twig rosemary
½ cup fresh parsley
¼ cup fresh thyme
½ tablespoon dried reishi mushrooms
½ tablespoon dried turkey tail mushrooms
½ tablespoon dried maitake mushrooms
½ tablespoon dried shiitake mushrooms
½ tablespoon dried dandelion
1 teaspoon powdered turmeric
1 teaspoon good quality salt
1 teaspoon pepper

Method:
Place everything in a large pot and bring to a boil. Reduce to low, cover with a lid, and simmer for 2–3 hours. Remove from heat, scoop into mug or bowl, and enjoy. This broth can be stored in the fridge for up to one week.

Tip: Consider adding some pressed and cubed organic tofu if you would prefer this drink to be a meal.

MEMORY (STRENGTHEN, RESTORE)

Memory is the power to retain and recall information and past experiences. Your brain's ability to support healthy cognitive processes help you recall more memories than if you were cognitively impaired. For example, people who suffer head injuries or live with dementia may have a more difficult time retrieving memories than someone who has not sustained brain injury from impact or disease.[31] Other common ways memory becomes disjointed include prolonged alcohol use and hormone changes.

Just as we place importance on supporting gut health or work to maintain healthy skin, we must also be intentional in supporting our brains and cognitive processes. The functional foods listed below help to sustain memory and overall brain health.

Helpful Foods
- Almond
- Avocado
- Coconut
- Echinacea
- Ginkgo
- Green tea
- Matcha

Ginkgo Echinacea Tea

Ingredients:
½ tablespoon dried ginkgo
½ tablespoon dried echinacea
1 cup filtered water
¼ teaspoon raw, unpasteurized honey (optional)

Method:
Heat water in kettle to at least 85°F. Combine dried herbs and steep in water, covered, for 10–15 minutes. Remove herbs from water, add honey if desired, and sip slowly.

Metabolic Syndrome (strengthen, restore)

Metabolic syndrome is a cluster of conditions or disorders, which include hypertension, insulin resistance, excess abdominal fat, and dyslipidemia (lipid imbalance). It's very common for some or all of these conditions to coexist in an individual with metabolic syndrome and increase the risk of type 2 diabetes, cardiovascular disease, and stroke.[32] This progressive disorder develops over many years and is difficult to reverse without intentional changes in one's diet, exercise regime, and general lifestyle.

Many plants have been shown to support the treatment of metabolic syndrome, and a plant-based lifestyle can help one overcome the health challenges associated with it in a big way.[33]

Helpful Foods
- Almond
- Blueberry
- Cashew
- Cinnamon
- Dandelion
- Ginseng
- Green tea
- Kale
- Oat
- Turmeric

BLUEBERRY GREEN TEA COOLER

Ingredients:
1 tablespoon green tea
1 cup filtered water
½ cup blueberries
1 cup ice
Pinch stevia

Method:
Heat water in kettle to at least 85°F. Steep green tea in water for 10–15 minutes. Remove herbs and set infused water aside to cool. Place blueberries in tall glass and smash with a spoon. Add ice, then pour cooled green tea over top. Add stevia if desired. Stir well, sip, and enjoy.

MORNING SICKNESS (SOOTHE)

Morning sickness refers to flu-like symptoms that many women feel during pregnancy. Some women experience nausea—especially upon waking—throughout their entire pregnancy, and for some it only lingers for their first trimester. Other women are lucky enough to skip this symptom of pregnancy altogether!

Among a few other plant-based gems, chamomile, ginger, lemon, and peppermint are all antiemetic and have been shown to improve the symptoms of morning sickness.[34] The fresh-pressed juice recipe associated with morning sickness is not only great for helping eradicate feelings of nausea but is also super healthy and full of much-needed vitamins, minerals, and antioxidants.

Helpful Foods
- Chamomile
- Ginger
- Lemon
- Peppermint

Fresh-Pressed Orange Ginger Juice

Ingredients:
1 thumb ginger
4 large carrots
1 apple
Squeeze of lemon

Method:
Clean all ingredients. Using your juicer, press ginger, carrots, and apple into a short glass. Squeeze fresh lemon over top and sip until it's gone. Repeat as necessary.

Tips: Make the night before and refrigerate in a sealed glass jar so it's ready the next morning for you to shake and sip immediately. If you can't stomach the smell of the ginger or carrots, try blending this juice with some ice to create a slushy or frozen drink. It will be less aromatic and more hydrating.

MOUTH ULCERS (SOOTHE)

Mouth ulcers are small sores that form on your lips, gums, inner cheeks, tongue, or roof of your mouth. A lot of different things can cause them, including spicy, salty, and acidic foods, minor injuries (such as accidentally biting your tongue), hormonal changes, and emotional stress. Most mouth ulcers go away on their own, and what we choose to consume can support the curative process and result in faster healing.

Helpful Foods
- Aloe
- Green tea
- Watermelon

Classic Green Tea

Ingredients:
1 tablespoon dried green tea
1 cup filtered water
¼ teaspoon raw, unpasteurized honey (optional)

Method:
Heat water in kettle to at least 85°F. Steep herbs in water, covered, for 10–15 minutes. Remove herbs or tea bag from water, add honey if desired, and sip slowly.

Tip: If you're making this tea several times a day to eradicate mouth ulcers, it might be worth it to purchase pre-portioned tea bags instead of using loose tea. Just keep in mind that quality counts. If you're a loose-tea lover, I recommend making a full pot of this tea and just keeping it on your counter so it's ready when you are.

Nausea (soothe)

Nausea is an uneasiness in your stomach that can often be accompanied by vomiting. It can be brought on by many things, such as motion sickness, pregnancy, flu, food poisoning, hangover, ear infection, cancer treatment, migraines, and low blood sugar. Luckily, there are a few tried-and-true plants that can make you feel better—if you can keep them down. The following healing and antiemetic recipe is to be sipped slowly and carefully. The goal is not to induce vomiting, but to slowly bring the stomach back to ease.

Helpful Foods
- Chamomile
- Ginger
- Lemon
- Peppermint

Warm Ginger Tonic with Lemon and Mint

Ingredients:
1½ cups water
1 small thumb fresh ginger, minced
1 tablespoon dried peppermint
½ lemon
¼ teaspoon raw, unpasteurized honey (optional)

Method:
Heat water in kettle to at least 85°F. Pour hot water into tea pot and add
ginger and mint leaves, steeping for at least 15 minutes. Remove stewed
herbs and pour into mug. Squeeze lemon over top and stir in honey if
desired. Sip slowly, adding some ice if you think a cooler temperature might
work better for you.

Tip: You can also use fresh mint if you have it, but I'd add a large handful to
the water instead of the smaller quantity required for dried mint.

Pain (Soothe)

Most of us fear pain, but pain is supposed to protect the body from what it perceives as real danger.[35] The International Association for the Study of Pain defines it as "an unpleasant sensory and emotional experience associated with actual or potential tissue damage or described in terms of such damage."[36]

There are two different types of pain: chronic and acute. Chronic pain is perceived regularly. Examples might include migraines, nerve pain, or arthritis. Acute pain is the opposite: pain that occurs suddenly and caused by injury, trauma, and illness. Examples of acute pain are labor and childbirth, broken bones, or an abscessed tooth. Many of the plants in this book that assist with pain are best for mild pain, not severe.

Helpful Foods
- Ginger
- Peppermint
- Turmeric

Ginger Turmeric Tea

Ingredients:
½ small thumb fresh ginger, peeled and grated
½ teaspoon powdered turmeric
1 cup filtered water
¼ teaspoon raw, unpasteurized honey (optional)

Method:
Heat water in kettle to at least 85°F. Combine turmeric with a bit of boiling water to create a thick paste. Add ginger and the remainder of water. Cover and steep for 10–15 minutes. Pour tea into a mug, add honey if desired, and sip slowly.

Tip: If this tea is too ginger-forward, try scooping out the little remnants. If you can, try to leave them in, as they are incredibly healing and good for the body.

Perimenopause (strengthen, restore)

Perimenopause (also simply known as peri) is a term used to describe the time leading up to menopause, which is defined as the absence of menses for twelve consecutive months. During peri, women experience declining hormone levels that lead to an array of symptoms that can be confusing, embarrassing, and downright annoying. This commonly starts anytime between the ages of 40–44[37] (though can certainly begin in the late 30s) and continues until menopause is achieved at the average age of 51.[38] I'm not going to lie: as someone currently going through this period of her life, I can personally attest to symptoms that can be frustrating and plentiful.

There are many medicinal herbs not listed in this book that are traditionally used for perimenopause and menopause symptoms. These include (but are not limited to) black cohosh, wild yam, red clover, dong quai, and ashwagandha. The following healing drink recipe associated with peri uses functional food to attempt to achieve the following: increased energy, cognition, and memory, and decreased inflammation, mood swings, and the risk of metabolic disorders.

Ladies, we're in this together. Drink up.

Helpful Foods
- Ginger
- Ginseng
- Green tea
- Kale
- Mushroom
- Oats
- Orange
- Turmeric

Orange Kale Smoothie

Ingredients:
1 cup kale, chopped
1 large orange, peeled and chopped
Small thumb of ginger, peeled and minced
½ cup unsweetened oat mylk
½ cup ice

Method:
Add all ingredients to blender and blend until smooth. Enjoy while cold and repeat daily if you can.

Tips: This smoothie is almost juice-like in its thinness. If you prefer a thicker smoothie, try freezing the peeled orange before using, or adding more ice. Swap oat mylk for cold green tea to diversify from time to time.

Premenstrual Syndrome (soothe)

Premenstrual syndrome (commonly known as PMS) is a term used to describe symptoms associated with women's impending periods. Typically, this starts during the luteal phase of the menstrual cycle—about a week or two prior to menstruation—and ends within a day or two of menses.[39] Symptoms can include headaches, abdominal bloating, acne, digestive changes, water retention, breast tenderness and/or swelling, mood swings, hot flashes, weight gain, and more.[40]

Bottom line? It's uncomfortable—so let's let food help us through it. The following list of foods have been shown to assist with PMS in a variety of ways. Mainly, they're anti-inflammatory, help reduce fluid retention, promote better sleep, and reduce general symptoms of hormonal hell.

Helpful Foods
- Avocado
- Beet
- Blueberry
- Cacao
- Carrot
- Fennel
- Oat
- Orange

Fennel Orange Tea

Ingredients:
1 tablespoon dried fennel
1 cup filtered water
½ orange

Method:
Heat water in kettle to at least 85°F. Steep fennel in water, covered, for 10–15 minutes. Remove fennel from water, squeeze fresh orange juice over top, and sip slowly.

Respiratory Health (strengthen)

Respiratory health refers to lung health. Aside from avoiding obvious things like smoking, vaping, and environmental pollutants, you can also challenge your cardiovascular system on a regular basis with vigorous exercise and eat healthfully to ensure a robust and disease-free respiratory system.

The plants associated with respiratory health are all superstars in their own ways. Some are expectorants, some promote and encourage deeper, healthier breathing, and some simply contain specific compounds that support general lung health.

Helpful Foods
- Aloe
- Cinnamon
- Citrus
- Echinacea
- Ginger
- Peppermint
- Rosemary
- Sage

WARMING ORANGE CINNAMON TEA

Ingredients:
½ orange, sliced with peel left intact
1 cinnamon stick
1 cup filtered water
¼ teaspoon raw, unpasteurized honey (optional)

Method:
Heat water in kettle to at least 85°F. Add orange and cinnamon, then steep, covered, for 10–15 minutes. Remove oranges and cinnamon, add honey if desired, and sip slowly.

Tip: If you love cinnamon, don't be afraid to leave a stick in your mug while you drink your tea—the scent is delicious.

Skin Health (strengthen)

The skin is the largest organ of the human body and it's not uncommon for underlying health issues to present themselves here. Strange skin discoloration, unexplained bruising, acute hives, and chronic acne are all clear signs that attention is required.

To help our skin remain as healthy as possible while both looking and feeling its best, we can turn to florals. Rose petals are well known for their anti-inflammatory activities and can be ingested as well as used topically to help improve skin deterioration.[41] Hibiscus has been proven to protect skin cells from oxidative stress, ultraviolet radiation, and collagen degradation.[42]

Helpful Foods
- Aloe
- Hibiscus
- Honey
- Rose
- Vanilla

Floral Cooler

Ingredients:
1 cup filtered water
½ tablespoon dried rose petals
½ tablespoon dried hibiscus buds
Raw, unpasteurized honey to taste (optional)
Thyme to garnish (optional)

Method:
Add rose petals and hibiscus buds to one cup of water. Set on counter at room temperature and let infuse for at least 15 minutes, stirring twice. Add honey if desired and stir until infused. Add ice to glass and pour infused water over top, straining as best you can. (Some floral remnants can stay in if you prefer.) Garnish with thyme, sip slowly, and enjoy.

Tip: Stir in honey while water is at least room temperature—if it's cool, the honey will not infuse well.

Stress (soothe)

Our modern world, full of light and sound pollution, consistent sensory overload, and general convenience puts great stress on our bodies. Add individual experiences into that crazy mix and we have a recipe for chronic stress. Unfortunately, stress is currently hypothesized to be one of the biggest predictors of disease in North America,[43] which means we need to do everything we can to lead peaceful lives to preserve our minds *and* our bodies.

Daily exercise and practicing mindfulness can work wonders for stress reduction, but food should not be ignored. Fermented foods are great for combatting stress.[44] Aside from miso, kombucha, apple cider vinegar, and fermented vegetables like sauerkraut and pickles are also great to incorporate into your diet. Try the foods on the list below and don't be afraid to experiment with your own recipes for stress relief—what works for others may not be what works best for you.

Helpful Foods
- Blueberry
- Chamomile
- Lavender
- Miso
- Mushroom
- Oat

Lavender Chamomile Tea

Ingredients:
½ tablespoon dried chamomile
½ tablespoon dried lavender
1 cup filtered water
¼ teaspoon raw, unpasteurized honey (optional)

Method:
Heat water in kettle to at least 85°F. Steep herbs in water, covered, for 10–15 minutes. Remove herbs or tea bag from water, add honey if desired, and sip slowly.

Tumors (strengthen, restore)

In a healthy body, our cells die when they grow old or become damaged, and new cells are created to take their place. Sometimes abnormal or damaged cells do not die, and instead they grow and multiply when they shouldn't. These cells may form tumors, which are essentially lumps of abnormal tissue. They can be malignant (cancerous) or benign (not cancerous).[45]

From a preventative perspective, there are certain medicinal foods we can consume that are especially good at thwarting abnormal cellular processes that may lead to tumor development. The foods listed below are all clinically cited to fall into the category of antitumor.

Helpful Foods
- Beet
- Mushroom
- Oat
- Peppermint
- Rosemary
- Turmeric
- Vanilla

TURMERIC OAT MYLK LATTE

Ingredients:
1 teaspoon powdered turmeric
1 tablespoon hot water
1 cup oat mylk
1 tablespoon raw, unpasteurized honey (optional)

Method:
Combine turmeric and hot water and stir into paste. Steam oat mylk until hot and frothy. Pour over top, add honey, and stir well. Enjoy!

Tip: As with our other recipes containing turmeric, I suggest following this recipe up with a glass of water and then brushing your teeth to avoid staining.

Urinary Tract Infections (soothe, restore)

Urinary tract infections (UTIs) are very common infections that occur when bacteria enter the urethra and infect the urinary tract. These infections can affect several parts of the urinary tract, but a bladder infection is the most common type. Women are much more prone to these infections than men.

Sometimes UTIs must be treated with antibiotics, but if you're familiar with the signs and symptoms and you catch the onset of infection quickly enough, it is totally possible to rid yourself of a UTI without medical intervention. Drinking lots of water and herbal cranberry teas can be very helpful, as they force urination, thereby flushing the urinary tract. You can also take cranberry supplements to both prevent and treat a UTI, as cranberries contain a substance that prevents infection from adhering to the walls of the bladder.[46] Note that conventional cranberry juice is not a good idea, as it typically contains a lot of sugar, and sugar feeds infection.

Helpful Foods
- Blueberry
- Cacao
- Cranberry
- Orange

Cranberry Orange Cooler

Ingredients:
½ cup fresh or previously frozen cranberries
½ orange, sliced
1 cup ice
2 cups water
Pinch stevia

Method:
Boil water in kettle to at least 100°F. Pour hot water into tea pot and add cranberries. Steep for at least 30 minutes. Place ice in a large glass. Remove berries and pour tea into the glass, over the ice. Add orange slices and stevia to taste and stir well. Consume 3 times per day for active infection, or once per day for preventative purposes.

Tip: Be sure to use stevia or another sugar alternative, as sugar could ultimately make a UTI worse.

WATER RETENTION (SOOTHE, RESTORE)

Water retention (also known as fluid retention or edema) is a buildup of excess fluid in the body. This issue can occur in cavities, tissues, and the circulatory system. The primary symptoms of water retention are swelling and a puffy, bloated appearance, and although common and relatively easy to treat most of the time, it can be associated with some serious conditions. Ways to relieve water retention include increasing mobility and movement, reducing sodium intake, and consuming foods that are diuretic and support kidney health.

Helpful Foods
- Celery
- Cranberry
- Dandelion
- Garlic
- Green tea
- Hibiscus
- Hops
- Onion
- Parsley
- Watermelon

Wild Dandelion Hops Tea

Ingredients:
½ tablespoon dried dandelion
½ tablespoon dried hops
1 cup filtered water
¼ teaspoon raw, unpasteurized honey (optional)

Method:
Heat water to at least 85°F. Steep herbs in water, covered, for 10–15 minutes. Remove herbs from water, add honey if desired, and sip slowly.

WEIGHT MANAGEMENT (RESTORE)

Trying to lose weight can be incredibly frustrating, and the older we get, the harder it can be to drop a few pounds. This can be related to the fact that our metabolism slows with age,[47] so we need to get creative to wake it up. Ways to help initiate positive metabolism shifts include a mixture of high and low intensity exercise, temperature fluctuations (such as finishing your daily shower with a burst of cold water), and intentional changes to what (and how) you are eating.

The following foods have been shown to positively support weight loss in a variety of ways, and the recipe provided is designed to wake up your body from the inside out.

Helpful Foods
- Aloe
- Cayenne
- Celery
- Cinnamon
- Dandelion
- Fennel
- Ginger
- Ginseng
- Hibiscus
- Lemon
- Parsley
- Peppermint
- Turmeric

Lemon Cayenne Tonic

Ingredients:
1 lemon
¼ teaspoon cayenne
2 cups filtered water
Ice (optional)
Celery for garnish (optional)

Method:
Place water in large jar. Squeeze juice from lemon into glass, then add cayenne. Place lid on jar and shake well. Add ice just before drinking, and celery to garnish (and eat) if you wish.

Acknowledgments

My sincerest thanks to Skyhorse Publishing and specifically to Abigail Gehring for her encouragement to work on this project.

Many hats off to shutterbug Chrissy Courtney for her artfulness, creativity, and ability to capture the most beautiful photographs. (And for helping me drink all the drinks.)

Also, a big thank you to Grant and Tycho, for selflessly allowing me to steal her for photo days.

Special shout out to Shawn for letting a stranger borrow mushrooms, ginseng, and very pretty hops for the purpose of lovely photos.

About the Author

Jennifer Browne is the author of several books published by Skyhorse Publishing, including her bestseller *The Good Living Guide to Medicinal Tea*. She has written extensively for a variety of wellness publications and is currently dabbling in contract writing and recipe development for various healthy food brands. Residing in British Columbia, she has a bachelor's degree in English Literature and a certificate in plant-based nutrition.

About the Photographer

Chrissy Courtney is a food photographer and graphic designer who dabbles in illustration. She lives in the British Columbian forest with her adventurous husband and her curious young son. When she is not making art, she meditates in the veggie garden, takes forest baths, and plays in the kitchen.

ENDNOTES

Introduction
1   Cotoraci, Coralia et al. "Natural antioxidants in anemia treatment."
    International journal of molecular sciences vol. 22,4 1883. 13 Feb. 2021,
    doi:10.3390/ijms22041883, https://www.ncbi.nlm.nih.gov/pmc/articles
    /PMC7918704/.
2   Bode AM, Dong Z. "The amazing and mighty ginger." In: Benzie IFF, Wachtel-
    Galor S, editors. *Herbal Medicine: Biomolecular and Clinical Aspects.* 2nd
    edition. Boca Raton (FL): CRC Press/Taylor & Francis; 2011. Chapter 7.
    Available from: https://www.ncbi.nlm.nih.gov/books/NBK92775/.

Bone Broth, Kefir, and Kombucha
1   Farag, Mohamed A et al. "The many faces of kefir fermented dairy products:
    Quality characteristics, flavour chemistry, nutritional value, health benefits,
    and safety." *Nutrients* vol. 12,2 346. 28 Jan. 2020, doi:10.3390/nu12020346.
2   de Miranda, Jeniffer Ferreira et al. "Kombucha: A review of substrates,
    regulations, composition, and biological properties." *Journal of Food Science*
    vol. 87,2 (2022): 503-527. doi:10.1111/1750-3841.16029.

Adaptogenic Mushrooms
1   Stamets, Paul, and Heather Zwickey. "Medicinal mushrooms: Ancient remedies
    meet modern science." *Integrative Medicine* (Encinitas, Calif.) vol. 13,1
    (2014): 46-7.

Sweeteners
1   Arnone, Djésia et al. "Sugars and gastrointestinal health." *Clinical
    Gastroenterology and Hepatology: the official clinical practice journal of the
    American Gastroenterological Association* vol. 20,9 (2022): 1912-1924.e7.
    doi:10.1016/j.cgh.2021.12.011.
2   Arumugam, Balakrishnan et al. "Stevia as a natural sweetener: A review."
    Cardiovascular & Hematological Agents in Medicinal Chemistry vol. 18,2
    (2020): 94-103. doi:10.2174/1871525718666200207105436.

3   Arumugam, Balakrishnan et al. "Stevia as a natural sweetener: A review."
     Cardiovascular & hematological agents in medicinal chemistry vol. 18,2 (2020):
     94-103. doi:10.2174/1871525718666200207105436.

4   Mandal, Manisha Deb, and Shyamapada Mandal. "Honey: Its medicinal
     property and antibacterial activity." *Asian Pacific journal of tropical biomedicine*
     vol. 1,2 (2011): 154-60. doi:10.1016/S2221-1691(11)60016-6.

5   Ibid.

6   Saraiva, Ariana et al. "Maple syrup: Chemical analysis and nutritional profile,
     health impacts, safety and quality control, and food industry applications."
     International Journal of Environmental Research and Public Health vol. 19,20
     13684. 21 Oct. 2022, doi:10.3390/ijerph192013684.

7   Ibid.

The Whole (Food) Story

1   Barreca, Davide et al. "Almonds (*Prunus Dulcis* Mill. D. A. Webb): A source of
     nutrients and health-promoting compounds." *Nutrients* vol. 12,3 672. 1 Mar.
     2020, doi:10.3390/nu12030672.

2   Dreher, Mark L. "A comprehensive review of almond clinical trials on
     weight measures, metabolic health biomarkers and outcomes, and the gut
     microbiota." *Nutrients* vol. 13,6 1968. 8 Jun. 2021, doi:10.3390/nu13061968.

3   Hekmatpou, Davood et al. "The effect of aloe vera clinical trials on prevention
     and healing of skin wound: A systematic review." *Iranian Journal of Medical
     Sciences* vol. 44,1 (2019): 1-9.

4   Foster M, Hunter D, Samman S. "Evaluation of the nutritional and metabolic
     effects of aloe vera." In: Benzie IFF, Wachtel-Galor S, editors. *Herbal Medicine:
     Biomolecular and Clinical Aspects*. 2nd edition. Boca Raton (FL): CRC Press/
     Taylor & Francis; 2011. Chapter 3. Available from: https://www.ncbi.nlm.nih
     .gov/books/NBK92765/.

5   Dreher, Mark L, and Adrienne J Davenport. "Hass avocado composition and
     potential health effects." *Critical Reviews in Food Science and Nutrition* vol.
     53,7 (2013): 738-50. doi:10.1080/10408398.2011.556759 https://pubmed
     .ncbi.nlm.nih.gov/23638933/.

6   Flores-Balderas, Ximena et al. "Beneficial effects of plant-based diets on skin
     health and inflammatory skin diseases." *Nutrients* vol. 15,13 2842. 22 Jun.
     2023, doi:10.3390/nu15132842 https://pubmed.ncbi.nlm.nih.gov
     /37447169/.

7   Dreher, Mark L et al. "A comprehensive review of hass avocado clinical trials,
     observational studies, and biological mechanisms." *Nutrients* vol. 13,12 4376.
     7 Dec. 2021, doi:10.3390/nu13124376.

8   Bensaid, Aicha et al. "Differential nutrition-health properties of *Ocimum basilicum* leaf and stem extracts." *Foods (Basel, Switzerland)* vol. 11,12 1699. 9 Jun. 2022, doi:10.3390/foods11121699.

9   Chen, Liping et al. "Beetroot as a functional food with huge health benefits: Antioxidant, antitumor, physical function, and chronic metabolomics activity." *Food Science & Nutrition* vol. 9,11 6406-6420. 9 Sep. 2021, doi:10.1002/fsn3.2577.

10   Gheith, I, and A El-Mahmoudy. "Laboratory evidence for the hematopoietic potential of *Beta vulgaris* leaf and stalk extract in a phenylhydrazine model of anemia." *Brazilian Journal of Medical and Biological Research = Revista brasileira de pesquisas medicas e biologicas* vol. 51,11 e7722. 11 Oct. 2018, doi:10.1590/1414-431X20187722.

11   Kalt, Wilhelmina et al. "Recent research on the health benefits of blueberries and their anthocyanins." *Advances in Nutrition (Bethesda, Md.)* vol. 11,2 (2020): 224-236. doi:10.1093/advances/nmz065.

12   Latif, Rabia. "Health benefits of cocoa." *Current Opinion in Clinical Nutrition and Metabolic Care* vol. 16,6 (2013): 669-74. doi:10.1097/MCO.0b013 e328365a235.

13   Soleti, Raffaella et al. "Carrot supplementation improves blood pressure and reduces aortic root lesions in an atherosclerosis-prone genetic mouse model." *Nutrients* vol. 13,4 1181. 2 Apr. 2021, doi:10.3390/nu13041181.

14   Ibid.

15   Khomich, L M et al. *Voprosy Pitaniia* vol. 89,1 (2020): 86-95. doi:10.24411/0042-8833-2020-10010.

16   Mah, Eunice et al. "Cashew consumption reduces total and LDL cholesterol: a randomized, crossover, controlled-feeding trial." *The American Journal of Clinical Nutrition* vol. 105,5 (2017): 1070-1078. doi:10.3945/ajcn.116.150037.

17   Ibid.

18   Sarabon, Nejc et al. "Acute effect of different concentrations of cayenne pepper cataplasm on sensory-motor functions and serum levels of inflammation-related biomarkers in healthy subjects." *European Journal of Translational Myology* vol. 28,1 7333. 1 Mar. 2018, doi:10.4081/ejtm.2018.7333.

19   "Cayenne." *University of Rochester Medical Center.* Web. Accessed 5 Oct. 2023. https://www.urmc.rochester.edu/encyclopedia/content.aspx?contenttypeid =19&contentid=Cayenne.

20   Hedayati, Narges et al. "Beneficial effects of celery (*Apium graveolens*) on metabolic syndrome: A review of the existing evidences." *Phytotherapy Research: PTR* vol. 33,12 (2019): 3040-3053. doi:10.1002/ptr.6492.

21   Ibid.

22   Dai, Yun-Lei et al. "Chamomile: A review of its traditional uses, chemical constituents, pharmacological activities and quality control studies." *Molecules*

(Basel, Switzerland) vol. 28,1 133. 23 Dec. 2022, doi:10.3390
/molecules28010133.

23 Ebrahimi, Peyman et al. "Chlorophylls as natural bioactive compounds existing
in food by-products: A critical review." *Plants (Basel, Switzerland)* vol. 12,7
1533. 2 Apr. 2023, doi:10.3390/plants12071533.

24 Kawatra, Pallavi, and Rathai Rajagopalan. "Cinnamon: Mystic powers of a
minute ingredient." *Pharmacognosy research* vol. 7, Suppl 1 (2015): S1-6.
doi:10.4103/0974-8490.157990.

25 Hewlings, Susan. "Coconuts and health: Different chain lengths of saturated
fats require different consideration." *Journal of Cardiovascular Development
and Disease* vol. 7,4 59. 17 Dec. 2020, doi:10.3390/jcdd7040059.

26 DebMandal, Manisha, and Shyamapada Mandal. "Coconut (*Cocos nucifera* L.:
Arecaceae): in health promotion and disease prevention." *Asian Pacific Journal
of Tropical Medicine* vol. 4,3 (2011): 241-7. doi:10.1016/S1995
-7645(11)60078-3.

27 Barrea, Luigi et al. "Coffee consumption, health benefits and side effects: a
narrative review and update for dietitians and nutritionists." *Critical Reviews in
Food Science and Nutrition* vol. 63,9 (2023): 1238-1261. doi:10.1080/104083
98.2021.1963207.

28 Xia, Jia-Yue et al. "Consumption of cranberry as adjuvant therapy for urinary
tract infections in susceptible populations: A systematic review and meta-
analysis with trial sequential analysis." *PloS one* vol. 16,9 e0256992. 2 Sep.
2021, doi:10.1371/journal.pone.0256992.

29 Bodet, C et al. "Potential oral health benefits of cranberry." *Critical
Reviews in Food Science and Nutrition* vol. 48,7 (2008): 672-80.
doi:10.1080/10408390701636211.

30 Epner, Margeaux et al. "Understanding the link between sugar and cancer: An
examination of the preclinical and clinical evidence." *Cancers* vol. 14,24 6042.
8 Dec. 2022, doi:10.3390/cancers14246042.

31 Mukherjee, Pulok K et al. "Phytochemical and therapeutic potential of
cucumber." *Fitoterapia* vol. 84 (2013): 227-36. doi:10.1016/j.fitote
.2012.10.003.

32 Kania-Dobrowolska, Małgorzata, and Justyna Baraniak. "Dandelion
(*Taraxacum officinale* L.) as a source of biologically active compounds
supporting the therapy of co-existing diseases in metabolic syndrome." *Foods
(Basel, Switzerland)* vol. 11,18 2858. 15 Sep. 2022, doi:10.3390/foods
11182858.

33 Percival, S S. "Use of echinacea in medicine." *Biochemical Pharmacology* vol.
60,2 (2000): 155-8. doi:10.1016/s0006-2952(99)00413-x.

34 Sharifi-Rad, Mehdi et al. "Echinacea plants as antioxidant and antibacterial
agents: From traditional medicine to biotechnological applications."

Phytotherapy Research: PTR vol. 32,9 (2018): 1653-1663. doi:10.1002/ptr
.6101.

35 Yakut, Halil Ibrahim et al. "Preventative and therapeutic effects of fennel
(*Foeniculum vulgare*) seed extracts against necrotizing enterocolitis." *Journal
of Food Biochemistry* vol. 44,8 (2020): e13284. doi:10.1111/jfbc.13284.

36 Ibid.

37 Nowak, Wioletta, and Małgorzata Jeziorek. "The role of flaxseed in improving
human health." *Healthcare (Basel, Switzerland)* vol. 11,3 395. 30 Jan. 2023,
doi:10.3390/healthcare11030395.

38 Ibid.

39 White, Danielle. "Healthy uses for garlic." *The Nursing clinics of North America*
vol. 56,1 (2021): 153-156. doi:10.1016/j.cnur.2020.12.001.

40 Bode AM, Dong Z. "The amazing and mighty ginger. In: Benzie IFF, Wachtel-
Galor S, editors. *Herbal Medicine: Biomolecular and Clinical Aspects.* 2nd
edition. Boca Raton (FL): CRC Press/Taylor & Francis; 2011. Chapter 7.
Available from: https://www.ncbi.nlm.nih.gov/books/NBK92775/.

41 Barbalho, Sandra Maria et al. "*Ginkgo biloba in the aging process: A narrative
review.*" *Antioxidants (Basel, Switzerland)* vol. 11,3 525. 9 Mar. 2022,
doi:10.3390/antiox11030525.

42 Ibid.

43 Cambria C, Sabir S, Shorter IC. "Ginseng." [Updated 2023 May 1]. In:
StatPearls [Internet]. *Treasure Island* (FL): *StatPearls Publishing*. Available
from: https://www.ncbi.nlm.nih.gov/books/NBK538198/.

44 Ibid.

45 Ibid.

46 Murphy, Mary M et al. "Consumption of grapefruit is associated with
higher nutrient intakes and diet quality among adults, and more favorable
anthropometrics in women, NHANES 2003-2008." *Food & Nutrition Research*
vol. 58 10.3402/fnr.v58.22179. 8 May. 2014, doi:10.3402/fnr.v58.22179.

47 Ibid.

48 Chacko, Sabu M et al. "Beneficial effects of green tea: A literature review."
Chinese Medicine vol. 5 13. 6 Apr. 2010, doi:10.1186/1749-8546-5-13.

49 Cabrera, Carmen et al. "Beneficial effects of green tea—a review." *Journal of
the American College of Nutrition* vol. 25,2 (2006): 79-99. doi:10.1080/07315
724.2006.10719518.

50 Ibid.

51 Dos Santos Nascimento, Luana Beatriz et al. "Phenolic compounds from leaves
and flowers of *Hibiscus roseus*: Potential skin cosmetic applications of an
under-investigated species." *Plants (Basel, Switzerland)* vol. 10,3 522. 10 Mar.
2021, doi:10.3390/plants10030522.

52 Jeffery, Tia D, and Matthew L Richardson. "A review of the effectiveness of hibiscus for treatment of metabolic syndrome." *Journal of Ethnopharmacology* vol. 270 (2021): 113762. doi:10.1016/j.jep.2020.113762.

53 Dos Santos Nascimento, Luana Beatriz et al. "Phenolic compounds from leaves and flowers of *Hibiscus roseus*: Potential skin cosmetic applications of an under-investigated species." *Plants (Basel, Switzerland)* vol. 10,3 522. 10 Mar. 2021, doi:10.3390/plants10030522.

54 Samarghandian, Saeed et al. "Honey and health: A review of recent clinical research." *Pharmacognosy Research* vol. 9,2 (2017): 121-127. doi:10.4103/0974-8490.204647.

55 Ibid.

56 Ibid.

57 Kyrou, Ioannis et al. "Effects of a hops (*Humulus lupulus* L.) dry extract supplement on self-reported depression, anxiety and stress levels in apparently healthy young adults: a randomized, placebo-controlled, double-blind, crossover pilot study." *Hormones (Athens, Greece)* vol. 16,2 (2017): 171-180. doi:10.14310/horm.2002.1738.

58 Ibid.

59 Ortega-Hernández, Erika et al. "Improving the health-benefits of kales (*Brassica oleracea* L. var. *acephala* DC) through the Application of Controlled Abiotic Stresses: A review." *Plants (Basel, Switzerland)* vol. 10,12 2629. 29 Nov. 2021, doi:10.3390/plants10122629.

60 Kim, Myoungsuk et al. "Effects of lavender on anxiety, depression, and physiological parameters: Systematic review and meta-analysis." *Asian Nursing Research* vol. 15,5 (2021): 279-290. doi:10.1016/j.anr. 2021.11.001 https://pubmed.ncbi.nlm.nih.gov/34775136.

61 Koulivand, Peir Hossein et al. "Lavender and the nervous system." *Evidence-Based Complementary and Alternative Medicine: eCAM* vol. 2013 (2013): 681304. doi:10.1155/2013/681304.

62 González-Molina, E et al. "Natural bioactive compounds of citrus limon for food and health." *Journal of Pharmaceutical and Biomedical Analysis* vol. 51,2 (2010): 327-45. doi:10.1016/j.jpba.2009.07.027.

63 Helen West, RD. "6 Evidence-Based Health Benefits of Lemons." *Healthline.* April 11, 2023.

64 Shimizu, Chikako et al. "Effects of lifelong intake of lemon polyphenols on aging and intestinal microbiome in the senescence-accelerated mouse prone 1 (SAMP1)." *Scientific Reports* vol. 9,1 3671. 6 Mar. 2019, doi:10.1038/s41598-019-40253-x.

65 Silva, Henrique, and Rita Bárbara. "Exploring the anti-hypertensive potential of lemongrass: a comprehensive review." *Biology* vol. 11,10 1382. 22 Sep. 2022, doi:10.3390/biology11101382.

66   Sokary, Sara et al. "The therapeutic potential of matcha tea: A critical review on human and animal studies." *Current Research in Food Science* vol. 6 100396. 23 Nov. 2022, doi:10.1016/j.crfs.2022.11.015.

67   Ibid.

68   Saeed, Farhan et al. "Miso: A traditional nutritious & health-endorsing fermented product." *Food Science & Nutrition* vol. 10,12 4103-4111. 15 Sep. 2022, doi:10.1002/fsn3.3029.

69   Panda, Sujogya Kumar, and Walter Luyten. "Medicinal mushrooms: Clinical perspective and challenges." *Drug discovery today* vol. 27,2 (2022): 636-651. doi:10.1016/j.drudis.2021.11.017.

70   Sang, Shengmin, and YiFang Chu. "Whole grain oats, more than just a fiber: Role of unique phytochemicals." *Molecular nutrition & food research* vol. 61,7 (2017): 10.1002/mnfr.201600715. doi:10.1002/mnfr.201600715.

71   Chen, Oliver et al. "The role of oat nutrients in the immune system: A narrative review." *Nutrients* vol. 13,4 1048. 24 Mar. 2021, doi:10.3390/nu13041048.

72   Griffiths, Gareth et al. "Onions—a global benefit to health." *Phytotherapy research: PTR* vol. 16,7 (2002): 603-15. doi:10.1002/ptr.1222.

73   Lv, Xinmiao et al. "Citrus fruits as a treasure trove of active natural metabolites that potentially provide benefits for human health." *Chemistry Central Journal* vol. 9 68. 24 Dec. 2015, doi:10.1186/s13065-015-0145-9.

74   Ibid.

75   Ibid.

76   Mahmood, Sidra et al. "Critique of medicinal conspicuousness of Parsley (*Petroselinum crispum*): a culinary herb of Mediterranean region." *Pakistan Journal of Pharmaceutical Sciences* vol. 27,1 (2014): 193-202.

77   Ibid.

78   Larijani, Bagher et al. "Prevention and treatment of flatulence from a traditional Persian medicine perspective." *Iranian Red Crescent Medical Journal* vol. 18,4 e23664. 31 Jan. 2016, doi:10.5812/ircmj.23664.

79   Chumpitazi, B P et al. "Review article: the physiological effects and safety of peppermint oil and its efficacy in irritable bowel syndrome and other functional disorders." *Alimentary pharmacology & therapeutics* vol. 47,6 (2018): 738-752. doi:10.1111/apt.14519.

80   McKay, Diane L, and Jeffrey B Blumberg. "A review of the bioactivity and potential health benefits of peppermint tea (*Mentha piperita* L.)." *Phytotherapy Research*: PTR vol. 20,8 (2006): 619-33. doi:10.1002/ptr.1936.

81   Mohd Ali, Maimunah et al. "Pineapple (*Ananas comosus*): A comprehensive review of nutritional values, volatile compounds, health benefits, and potential food products." *Food Research International* (Ottawa, Ont.) vol. 137 (2020): 109675. doi:10.1016/j.foodres.2020.109675.

82 Lee, Myung-Hee et al. "Skin anti-inflammatory activity of rose petal extract (*Rosa gallica*) through reduction of MAPK signaling pathway." *Food Science & Nutrition* vol. 6,8 2560-2567. 25 Oct. 2018, doi:10.1002/fsn3.870.

83 Mohebitabar, Safieh et al. "Therapeutic efficacy of rose oil: A comprehensive review of clinical evidence." *Avicenna journal of phytomedicine* vol. 7,3 (2017): 206-213.

84 Ghasemzadeh Rahbardar, Mahboobeh, and Hossein Hosseinzadeh. "Therapeutic effects of rosemary (*Rosmarinus officinalis* L.) and its active constituents on nervous system disorders." *Iranian Journal of Basic Medical Sciences* vol. 23,9 (2020): 1100-1112. doi:10.22038/ijbms.2020.45269.10541.

85 Ibid.

86 Ibid.

87 Ibid.

88 Li Pomi, Federica et al. "*Rosmarinus officinalis* and skin: Antioxidant activity and possible therapeutical role in cutaneous diseases." *Antioxidants* (Basel, Switzerland) vol. 12,3 680. 9 Mar. 2023, doi:10.3390/antiox12030680.

89 Hammoudi Halat, Dalal et al. "A focused insight into thyme: Biological, chemical, and therapeutic properties of an indigenous Mediterranean herb." *Nutrients* vol. 14,10 2104. 18 May. 2022, doi:10.3390/nu14102104.

90 Nieto, Gema. "A review on applications and uses of thymus in the food industry." *Plants (Basel, Switzerland)* vol. 9,8 961. 30 Jul. 2020, doi:10.3390/plants9080961.

91 Hewlings, Susan J, and Douglas S Kalman. "Curcumin: A review of its effects on human health." *Foods (Basel, Switzerland)* vol. 6,10 92. 22 Oct. 2017, doi:10.3390/foods6100092.

92 Ibid.

93 Shanmugam, Muthu K et al. "The multifaceted role of curcumin in cancer prevention and treatment." *Molecules (Basel, Switzerland)* vol. 20,2 2728-69. 5 Feb. 2015, doi:10.3390/molecules20022728.

94 Kim, Mi Eun et al. "Anti-neuroinflammatory effects of vanillin through the regulation of inflammatory factors and NF-κB signaling in LPS-stimulated microglia." *Applied Biochemistry and Biotechnology* vol. 187,3 (2019): 884-893. doi:10.1007/s12010-018-2857-5.

95 Arya, Sagar S. et al. "Vanillin: a review on the therapeutic prospects of a popular flavouring molecule." *Advances in Traditional Medicine* vol. 21,3 (2021): 1–17. doi:10.1007/s13596-020-00531-w.

96 Ibid.

97 Manivannan, Abinaya et al. "Versatile nutraceutical potentials of watermelon: a modest fruit loaded with pharmaceutically valuable phytochemicals." *Molecules (Basel, Switzerland)* vol. 25,22 5258. 11 Nov. 2020, doi:10.3390/molecules25225258.

Healing Recipes

1   "What is anemia?" *NIH*. 24 March 2022. Accessed on 2 October 2023. https://www.nhlbi.nih.gov/health/anemia.

2   Piskin, Elif et al. "Iron absorption: Factors, limitations, and improvement methods." *ACS Omega* 2022 7 (24), 20441-20456 DOI: 10.1021/acsomega.2c01833. https://pubs.acs.org/doi/10.1021/acsomega.2c01833.

3   Domínguez, Raúl et al. "Effects of beetroot juice supplementation on cardiorespiratory endurance in athletes. A systematic review." *Nutrients* vol. 9,1 43. 6 Jan. 2017, doi:10.3390/nu9010043.

4   Chand SP, Marwaha R. "Anxiety." [Updated 2023 Apr 24]. In: *StatPearls* [Internet]. Treasure Island (FL): *StatPearls Publishing*. Available from: https://www.ncbi.nlm.nih.gov/books/NBK470361/.

5   Hashmi MF, Tariq M, Cataletto ME. "Asthma." [Updated 2023 Aug 8]. In: *StatPearls* [Internet]. Treasure Island (FL): *StatPearls Publishing*. Available from: https://www.ncbi.nlm.nih.gov/books/NBK430901/.

6   Ibid.

7   Amaral-Machado, Lucas et al. "Use of natural products in asthma treatment." *Evidence-Based Complementary and Alternative Medicine: eCAM* vol. 2020 1021258. 13 Feb. 2020, doi:10.1155/2020/1021258.

8   Foley, Anna et al. "Management strategies for abdominal bloating and distension." *Gastroenterology & Hepatology* vol. 10,9 (2014): 561-71.

9   Ozemek, Cemal et al. "The role of diet for prevention and management of hypertension." *Current Opinion in Cardiology* vol. 33,4 (2018): 388-393. doi:10.1097/HCO.0000000000000532.

10   Hemilä, H. "Vitamin C and the common cold." *The British Journal of Nutrition* vol. 67,1 (1992): 3-16. doi:10.1079/bjn19920004.

11   Shrimanker I, Bhattarai S. Electrolytes. [Updated 2023 Jul 24]. In: *StatPearls* [Internet]. Treasure Island (FL): *StatPearls Publishing*. Available from: https://www.ncbi.nlm.nih.gov/books/NBK541123/.

12   Chand, Suma P. and Hasan Arif. "Depression." *StatPearls*, *StatPearls Publishing*, 17 July 2023.

13   Xi, Pan, and Rui Hai Liu. "Whole food approach for type 2 diabetes prevention." *Molecular Nutrition & Food Research* vol. 60,8 (2016): 1819-36. doi:10.1002/mnfr.201500963.

14   Smirmaul, Bruno P C et al. "Effects of caffeine on neuromuscular fatigue and performance during high-intensity cycling exercise in moderate hypoxia." *European Journal of Applied Physiology* vol. 117,1 (2017): 27-38. doi:10.1007/s00421-016-3496-6 https://pubmed.ncbi.nlm.nih.gov/27864638/.

15   Dreher, Mark L. "A comprehensive review of almond clinical trials on weight measures, metabolic health biomarkers and outcomes, and the gut

microbiota." *Nutrients* vol. 13,6 1968. 8 Jun. 2021, doi:10.3390/nu13061968 https://pubmed.ncbi.nlm.nih.gov/34201139/.

16   Saeed, Farhan et al. "Miso: A traditional nutritious & health-endorsing fermented product." *Food Science & Nutrition* vol. 10,12 4103-4111. 15 Sep. 2022, doi:10.1002/fsn3.3029.

17   Feller, L, and E Blignaut. "Halitosis: a review." *SADJ: Journal of the South African Dental Association = tydskrif van die Suid-Afrikaanse Tandheelkundige Vereniging* vol. 60,1 (2005): 17-9.

18   Wiese, J G et al. "The alcohol hangover." *Annals of Internal Medicine* vol. 132,11 (2000): 897-902. doi:10.7326/0003-4819-132-11-200006060-00008.

19   Herdiana, Yedi. "Functional food in relation to gastroesophageal reflux disease (GERD)." *Nutrients* vol. 15,16 3583. 15 Aug. 2023, doi:10.3390/nu15163583.

20   Ibid.

21   Wiertsema, Selma P et al. "The interplay between the gut microbiome and the immune system in the context of infectious diseases throughout life and the role of nutrition in optimizing treatment strategies." *Nutrients* vol. 13,3 886. 9 Mar. 2021, doi:10.3390/nu13030886 https://pubmed.ncbi.nlm.nih.gov/33803407/.

22   Carr, Anitra C, and Silvia Maggini. "Vitamin C and immune function." *Nutrients* vol. 9,11 1211. 3 Nov. 2017, doi:10.3390/nu9111211.

23   Chen, Oliver et al. "The role of oat nutrients in the immune system: A narrative review." *Nutrients* vol. 13,4 1048. 24 Mar. 2021, doi:10.3390/nu13041048 https://www.ncbi.nlm.nih.gov/pmc/articles/PMC8063794/.

24   Chen, Linlin et al. "Inflammatory responses and inflammation-associated diseases in organs." *Oncotarget* vol. 9,6 7204-7218. 14 Dec. 2017, doi:10.18632/oncotarget.23208.

25   "Lavender." *Drugs and Lactation Database* (LactMed®), *National Institute of Child Health and Human Development*, 15 September 2023. https://pubmed.ncbi.nlm.nih.gov/30000925/.

26   Freeman, Andrew M., et al. "Insulin resistance." *StatPearls, StatPearls Publishing*, 17 August 2023.

27   Gołąbek, Katarzyna Daria, and Bożena Regulska-Ilow. "Dietary support in insulin resistance: An overview of current scientific reports." *Advances in Clinical and Experimental Medicine: Official Organ Wroclaw Medical University* vol. 28,11 (2019): 1577-1585. doi:10.17219/acem/109976.

28   Ogobuiro I, Tuma F. Physiology, Renal. [Updated 2023 Jul 24]. In: *StatPearls* [Internet]. Treasure Island (FL): *StatPearls Publishing*. Available from: https://www.ncbi.nlm.nih.gov/books/NBK538339/.

29   "Hops." *Drugs and Lactation Database* (LactMed®) [Internet]. Bethesda (MD): *National Institute of Child Health and Human Development*; 2006.

[Updated 2021 Feb 15]. Available from: https://www.ncbi.nlm.nih.gov /books/NBK501833/.

30 "Liver." *Cleveland Clinic*. Accessed 9 Dec. 2023. Web. https://my .clevelandclinic.org/health/articles/21481-liver.

31 Dröes, Rose-Marie et al. "Memory problems in dementia: adaptation and coping strategies and psychosocial treatments." *Expert Review of Neurotherapeutics* vol. 11,12 (2011): 1769-81; quiz 1782. doi:10.1586 /ern.11.167.

32 Graf, Brittany L et al. "Plant-derived therapeutics for the treatment of metabolic syndrome." *Current Opinion in Investigational Drugs* (London, England : 2000) vol. 11,10 (2010): 1107-15.

33 Thomas, Minu S et al. "Healthy plant-based diets improve dyslipidemias, insulin resistance, and inflammation in metabolic syndrome. A narrative review." *Advances in Nutrition* (Bethesda, Md.) vol. 14,1 (2023): 44-54. doi:10.1016/j.advnut.2022.10.002.

34 Khorasani, Fahimeh et al. "A systematic review of the efficacy of alternative medicine in the treatment of nausea and vomiting of pregnancy." *Journal of Obstetrics and Gynaecology: the Journal of the Institute of Obstetrics and Gynaecology* vol. 40,1 (2020): 10-19. doi:10.1080/01443615.2019.1587392.

35 Mankelow J, Ryan CG, Green PW, Taylor PC, Martin D. "An exploration of primary care healthcare professionals' understanding of pain and pain management following a brief pain science education." *BMC Medical Education*. 2022 Mar 28;22(1):211.

36 Treede, Rolf-Detlef. "The international association for the study of pain definition of pain: as valid in 2018 as in 1979, but in need of regularly updated footnotes." *Pain Reports* vol. 3,2 e643. 5 Mar. 2018, doi:10.1097/ PR9.0000000000000643.

37 Tarlatzis, Basil C, and Leonidas Zepiridis. "Perimenopausal conception." *Annals of the New York Academy of Sciences* vol. 997 (2003): 93-104. doi:10.1196 /annals.1290.011.

38 Peacock K, Ketvertis KM. Menopause. [Updated 2022 Aug 11]. In: *StatPearls* [Internet]. Treasure Island (FL): *StatPearls Publishing*. Available from: https: //www.ncbi.nlm.nih.gov/books/NBK507826/.

39 Dickerson, Lori M et al. "Premenstrual syndrome." *American Family Physician* vol. 67,8 (2003): 1743-52.

40 Ibid.

41 Lee, Myung-Hee et al. "Skin anti-inflammatory activity of rose petal extract (*Rosa gallica*) through reduction of MAPK signaling pathway." *Food Science & Nutrition* vol. 6,8 2560-2567. 25 Oct. 2018, doi:10.1002/fsn3.870 https: //www.ncbi.nlm.nih.gov/pmc/articles/PMC6261181/.

42 Dos Santos Nascimento, Luana Beatriz et al. "Phenolic compounds from leaves and flowers of *hibiscus roseus*: Potential skin cosmetic applications of an under-investigated species." *Plants (Basel, Switzerland)* vol. 10,3 522. 10 Mar. 2021, doi:10.3390/plants10030522 https://www.ncbi.nlm.nih.gov/pmc/articles/PMC8000889.

43 Salleh, Mohd Razali. "Life event, stress and illness." *The Malaysian Journal of Medical Sciences: MJMS* vol. 15,4 (2008): 9-18.

44 Naidoo, Uma. "Eat to Beat Stress." *American Journal of Lifestyle Medicine* vol. 15,1 39-42. 8 Dec. 2020, doi:10.1177/1559827620973936.

45 "What is cancer?" *National Cancer Institute*. 11 Oct. 2021. Accessed 15 Nov. 2023. https://www.cancer.gov/about-cancer/understanding/what-is-cancer.

46 Williams, Gabrielle et al. "Cranberries for p+reventing urinary tract infections." *The Cochrane Database of Systematic Reviews* vol. 4,4 CD001321. 17 Apr. 2023, doi:10.1002/14651858.CD001321.pub6.

47 Roberts, Susan B, and Irwin Rosenberg. "Nutrition and aging: Changes in the regulation of energy metabolism with aging." *Physiological Reviews* vol. 86,2 (2006): 651-67. doi:10.1152/physrev.00019.2005.

Index